Supporting Users and Troubleshooting Desktop Applications on a Microsoft® Windows® XP Operating System (70-272)

Lab Manual

Owen Fowler

PUBLISHED BY
Microsoft Press
A Division of Microsoft Corporation
One Microsoft Way
Redmond, Washington 98052-6399

Library of Congress Cataloging-in-Publication Data

Printed and bound in the United States of America.

3 4 5 6 7 8 9   QWT   9 8 7 6 5 4

A CIP catalogue record for this book is available from the British Library.

Microsoft Press books are available through booksellers and distributors worldwide. For further information about international editions, contact your local Microsoft Corporation office or contact Microsoft Press International directly at fax (425)
936-7329. Visit our Web site at www.microsoft.com/learning/. Send comments to *mspinput@microsoft.com*.

Acquisitions Editor: Linda Engelman
Project Editor: Barbara Moreland
Technical Editor: Robert Brunner

ISBN 13: 978-0-470-64114-9

SubAssy Part No. X10-58434
Body Part No. X10-58437

CONTENTS

LAB 1: Preliminary Tasks and Understanding Technical Support Tiers 1

Before You Begin..1

Scenario..1

Exercise 1.1: Activating Windows 2

Exercise 1.2: Demoting Your Student Account to User Level 2

Exercise 1.3: Determining Network Membership 3

Exercise 1.4: Taking a Screen Shot...........................4

Exercise 1.5: Copying the Lab Manual Folder to Shared Documents..5

Exercise 1.6: Creating a Test User Account 5

Lab Review Questions 6

Lab Challenge: Assigning Tasks in a Technical Support Environment 6

LAB 2: Resolving Service Calls 7

Scenario..7

Exercise 2.1: Role-Playing: Troubleshooting a Printing Problem 8

    Creating the Problem....................................8

    Asking Questions 9

    Re-Creating the Problem 9

    Using Help And Support to Find a Solution 10

    Implementing the Solution 12

    Testing the Solution....................................13

Exercise 2.2: Role-Playing: Troubleshooting a Graphics Problem 14

    Creating the DirectX Problem 14

    Asking Questions 16

    Testing the Problem with Dxdiag.exe......................16

    Implementing the Solution 18

    Testing the Solution....................................18

Exercise 2.3: Finding Solutions at the Microsoft Knowledge Base 18

Exercise 2.4: Finding Solutions at Microsoft TechNet 20

Lab Review Questions 21

Lab Challenge: Creating a Technical Support Documentation Form 21

LAB 3: **Simple Microsoft Windows XP Configuration Issues . . .23**

Scenario. 23

Exercise 3.1: Configuring the Notification Area 24

    Modifying Icon Behavior in the Notification Area. 24

    Restoring the Notification Area Defaults 25

Exercise 3.2: Configuring Startup Applications. 25

Exercise 3.3: Configuring Quick Launch. 26

Exercise 3.4: Configuring the Taskbar. .28

    Adding a Desktop Toolbar to the Taskbar. 28

    Adding a Favorites Toolbar to the Taskbar 29

    Adding a Network Share Toolbar to the Taskbar. 29

Exercise 3.5: Configuring the Start Menu 30

    Adding the Woodgrove Bank Program Group to All Programs 30

    Moving the Windows Update Shortcut from All Programs
    to the Start Menu 31

    Adding the Network Connections Folder and Administrative
    Tools to the Start Menu. 32

Exercise 3.6: Configuring Input Languages 32

    Assigning Russian as the Input Language 32

    Removing the Alt + Shift Language Toggle Option. 33

Exercise 3.7: Configuring Folder Settings 34

Exercise 3.8: Changing File Associations 35

Exercise 3.9: Using Disk Maintenance Utilities 35

Lab Review Questions 36

Lab Challenge: Creating a Custom Desktop. 37

LAB 4: **Microsoft Outlook and Outlook Express. 39**

Before You Begin. 39

Scenario. 40

Exercise 4.1: Installing Microsoft Office Outlook 2003 40

Exercise 4.2: Configuring Microsoft Outlook as a POP3
Mail Client 41

Exercise 4.3: Configuring Microsoft Outlook as an IMAP
Mail Client 43

Exercise 4.4: Configuring .PST File Locations 44

Exercise 4.5: Backing Up Outlook Data. 46

Exercise 4.6: Common Configuration Options in Outlook 47

    Disable Send Immediately When Connected 48

    Enable Leave Messages On Server. .48

    Using Plain Text to Create Messages 49

    Enable Automatic Download of Images in E-Mails 49

    Limiting Junk E-Mail. 50

Exercise 4.7: Configuring a Newsgroup Client in Outlook Express . . .50

Exercise 4.8: Maintaining Outlook 51

    Emptying Deleted Items Folder on Exiting 51

    Setting Automatic Archiving Options .52

    Compacting Outlook Data 53

Lab Review Questions 53

Lab Challenge: Configuring Outlook Express as an E-Mail Client 54

LAB 5:   Configuring Internet Explorer 55

Before You Begin. 55

Scenario. 55

Exercise 5.1: Setting a Home Page. 56

Exercise 5.2: Configuring Accessibility 57

    Enlarging Text Size 57

    Changing Fonts. 58

    Changing Colors 58

    Changing Toolbar Icon Sizes. 59

Exercise 5.3: Adding Languages (Optional) 59

Exercise 5.4: Viewing History (Optional) 60

    Changing History Order 60

    Deleting and Configuring the History List. 61

Exercise 5.5: Common Settings 61

    Related Information Button 61

    Accessing Folders from Internet Explorer. 62

    Starting Internet Explorer with a Blank Home Page. 62

    Configuring the Search Toolbar. 63

Exercise 5.6: Managing Favorites 64

    Adding Items to Favorites. 64

    Manually Editing Favorites 64

    Configuring a Favorite for Offline Use .65

    Importing Favorites 66

Exercise 5.7: Using Group Policy Settings for Internet Explorer 67

Exercise 5.8: Maintaining Internet Explorer 68

    Deleting Temporary Internet Files Manually 69

    Automatically Deleting Temporary Internet Files on Exiting
    Internet Explorer 69

    Deleting Cookies. 70

    Changing the Cached Pages Update Settings 70

Exercise 5.9: Securing Internet Explorer 70

    Configuring Security Zones. 71

    Setting Cookie Options to Secure Privacy 72

Exercise 5.10: Submitting Your Work 72

Lab Review Questions 72

Lab Challenge 5.1: Configuring Internet Explorer to
Work with Other Programs 73
Lab Challenge 5.2: Customizing Security Zones 73

LAB 6: **Installing and Configuring the Microsoft Office System . . 75**
Before You Begin 75
Scenario 76
Exercise 6.1: Checking System Requirements Using Msinfo32 76
Exercise 6.2: Creating and Using a System Restore Point 77
Exercise 6.3: Installing Microsoft Office Professional
Edition 2003 79
Exercise 6.4: Configuring Program Compatibility 80
Exercise 6.5: Adding and Using a Toolbar 81
Exercise 6.6: Creating a Custom Toolbar 82
Exercise 6.7: Configuring Microsoft Word 83
    Creating a New Document from a Template 83
    Viewing Formatting Marks 84
    Altering Selection Behavior 84
    Changing Printing Settings 84
    Changing File Locations to a Network Share 85
    Altering Markup Settings 85
    Configuring Proofing Tools 85
    Configuring AutoCorrect Options 86
Exercise 6.8: Adding Items to a Menu List 87
Exercise 6.9: Submitting Your Work 87
Lab Review Questions 88
Lab Challenge: Configuring a Group Project for
Microsoft Office Excel 2003 88

LAB 7: **Troubleshooting Office Applications 89**
Before You Begin 89
Scenario 89
Exercise 7.1: Restoring Default Menu Settings in
Word 2003 90
Exercise 7.2: Removing Unneeded Components from
Microsoft Office 91
Exercise 7.3: Changing Language Formats 92
Exercise 7.4: Creating a Chart in Excel 93
Exercise 7.5: Creating and Modifying an Excel Macro 94
    Creating a Macro in Excel 94
    Editing a Macro in Visual Basic 95
Exercise 7.6: Embedding and Linking Objects in Excel 96
Exercise 7.7: Opening and Repairing an Office File 97
Exercise 7.8: Using Microsoft Office Application Recovery 98

Exercise 7.9: Configuring Backup and Recovery Settings 99

Exercise 7.10: Submitting Your Work 100

Lab Review Questions 100

Lab Challenge: Linking and Embedding Objects in PowerPoint. 101

TROUBLESHOOTING LAB A: **Reviewing Your Environment** **103**

Lab Dependencies 104

Changing the Computer Configuration. 104

Troubleshooting. 104

Break Scenario 1 104

Break Scenario 2 105

Break Scenario 3 106

LAB 8:   **Configuring and Troubleshooting Connectivity.** **109**

Before You Begin. 110

Scenario. 110

Exercise 8.1: Configuring an Internet Connection. 110

Exercise 8.2: Installing a Modem (Optional) 111

Exercise 8.3: Querying a Modem from Modem
Properties (Optional) 112

Exercise 8.4: Common Modem Settings (Optional) 113

Turning Off the Speaker and Enabling Error Correction
and Flow Control 114

Disabling Hang-up When Idle 114

Exercise 8.5: Changing Workgroups 115

Exercise 8.6: Using the Repair Feature for Network Connections. . .116

Exercise 8.7: Obtaining an Automatic Private IP Address 118

Exercise 8.8: Joining a Domain 118

Exercise 8.9: Using Network Diagnostics in the
Help And Support Center 120

Exercise 8.10: Using Ping 122

Exercise 8.11: Using Tracert, Pathping, and NSlookup 123

Using Pathping 123

Using Tracert 124

Using NSlookup 124

Exercise 8.12: Restoring the System for Future Labs 124

Exercise 8.13: Submitting Your Work 125

Exercise 8.14: Installing Microsoft ActiveSync
(Optional) 125

Exercise 8.15: Setting Up a Partnership and
Synchronizing a Pocket PC (Optional) 127

Exercise 8.16: Dealing with Synchronization
Conflicts (Optional) 128

Lab Review Questions 130

Lab Challenge 8.1: Using the Command Line to
Troubleshoot a Connection Failure .130

Lab Challenge 8.2: Synchronization Preferences 131

LAB 9: **Security and Sharing in Windows XP
Professional** **133**

Before You Begin. 133

Adding Your Computer to the Correct Workgroup 133

Scenario. 134

Exercise 9.1: Sharing a Document Locally. 134

Exercise 9.2: Sharing Folders in a Workgroup Using
Simple File Sharing 135

Exercise 9.3: Making a Folder Private 136

Exercise 9.4: Sharing Folders in a Workgroup Without
Simple File Sharing 136

Exercise 9.5: Setting NTFS Permissions on a Shared
Network Folder 138

Exercise 9.6: Adding a User to the Backup Operators Group. 140

Exercise 9.7: Setting Password Policies 140

Exercise 9.8: Setting Lockout Policies. 141

Exercise 9.9: Assigning User Rights 142

Exercise 9.10: Configuring Security Options 143

Exercise 9.11: Configuring Group Policy in a Workgroup 144

Lab Review Questions 144

Lab Challenge: Determining Resultant User Rights. 144

LAB 10: **Updating and Protecting Windows XP
Professional** **147**

Before You Begin. 147

Adding Your Computer to the Correct Workgroup 147

Scenario. 148

Exercise 10.1: Manually Updating Windows 148

Exercise 10.2: Enabling ICF 150

Exercise 10.3: Enabling an ICMP Component 151

Exercise 10.4: Logging with ICF 152

Exercise 10.5: Starting a Service Within ICF 154

Exercise 10.6: Removing ICF 154

Exercise 10.7: Installing MBSA 155

Exercise 10.8: Using MBSA 155

Exercise 10.9: Submitting Your Work .156

Lab Review Questions 157

Lab Challenge: Automating Windows Update 157

LAB 11: Multiuser and Multiboot Computers **159**

Before You Begin. 159

Adding Your Computer to the Correct Workgroup 159

Scenario. 160

Exercise 11.1: Adding User Accounts to Multiuser
Computers in a Workgroup. 160

Adding a Power User Account 161

Adding a Guest Account. 162

Exercise 11.2: Sharing Applications on a Multiuser Computer. 163

Exercise 11.3: Configuring Boot Options on a
Multiboot Computer. 165

Exercise 11.4: Configuring Program Compatibility Settings 165

Exercise 11.5: Using Remote Desktop 166

Lab Review Questions 167

Lab Challenge: Resolving File Ownership Problems
After an Upgrade to Windows XP. 167

TROUBLESHOOTING LAB B: Reviewing Your Environment **169**

Lab Dependencies 170

Changing the Computer Configuration 170

Troubleshooting 170

Break Scenario 1 170

Break Scenario 2 172

LAB 1

PRELIMINARY TASKS AND UNDERSTANDING TECHNICAL SUPPORT TIERS

This lab contains the following exercises and activities:

■ **Exercise 1.1: Activating Windows**

■ **Exercise 1.2: Demoting Your Student Account to User Level**

■ **Exercise 1.3: Determining Network Membership**

■ **Exercise 1.4: Taking a Screen Shot**

■ **Exercise 1.5: Copying the Lab Manual Folder to Shared Documents**

■ **Exercise 1.6: Creating a Test User Account**

■ **Lab Review Questions**

■ **Lab Challenge: Assigning Tasks in a Technical Support Environment**

BEFORE YOU BEGIN

Lab 1 assumes that setup has been completed as specified in the setup document, and that your computer has connectivity to other lab computers and the Internet (Internet access might be restricted).

SCENARIO

In this lab you are asked to complete tasks that are necessary for completing subsequent labs. Therefore, some of the exercises in this first lab are mandatory. These exercises include the following:

■ Exercise 1.1: Activating Windows

■ Exercise 1.2: Demoting Your Student Account to User Level

■ Exercise 1.5: Copying the Lab Manual Folder to Shared Documents

■ Exercise 1.6: Creating a Test User Account

In the Lab Challenge, you are asked to put yourself in the role of an administrator designing a technical support tier structure for Proseware, Inc., a company that specializes in supporting video games.

After completing this lab, you will be able to:

- Activate the Microsoft Windows XP operating system.
- Identify to what type of network a Microsoft Windows XP Professional workstation belongs.
- Take both a full and active-window screen shot.
- Demote an Administrator Account.
- Create a User Account.

Estimated lesson time: 45 minutes

EXERCISE 1.1: ACTIVATING WINDOWS

Estimated completion time: 5 minutes

In the following steps, you will activate Windows XP over the Internet.

1. From the Start menu, choose All Programs, Accessories, System Tools, and select Activate Windows.

2. In the Activate Windows wizard, on the Let's Activate Windows page, select Yes, Let's Activate Windows Over The Internet Now. Click Next.

3. On the Register With Microsoft? page, select No, I Don't Want To Register Now; Let's Just Activate Windows. Click Next.

4. On the Thank You page, click OK. Windows is now activated.

EXERCISE 1.2: DEMOTING YOUR STUDENT ACCOUNT TO USER LEVEL

Estimated completion time: 5 minutes

For security, it is best to use an account with the least privileges possible for any task. Therefore, in this exercise, you will demote your student account to the User security level. You will use an administrator account for tasks when the user account's security privileges are insufficient.

In the following steps, you will lower the security level of your student account to the User level.

1. From the Start menu, right-click My Computer, and then select Manage.

2. In the Computer Management console, expand System Tools, and then select Local Users And Groups.

3. In the details pane, double-click Users, and then double-click Student*xx* (where Student*xx* is your student account user name).

4. In Student*xx* Properties, in the Member Of tab, click Add.

5. In the Select Groups dialog box, click Advanced.

6. In the second Select Groups dialog box, click Find Now.

7. In the search results list box, select Users, as shown below, and then click OK.

8. In the first Select Groups dialog box, click OK.

9. In Student*xx* Properties, in the Member Of list box, select Administrators, click Remove, and then click OK.

10. Close the Computer Management console.

11. From the Start menu, select Log Off. In the Log Off Windows box, click Log Off.

QUESTION   What are the two user names available for logging on?

EXERCISE 1.3: DETERMINING NETWORK MEMBERSHIP

Estimated completion time: 5 minutes

When troubleshooting a computer problem in a networked environment, it is sometimes important to determine to what type of network a computer belongs.

In the following task, you will determine to what type of network your Windows XP Professional installation belongs, using two different methods.

1. Log on to Windows XP Professional with your student account.

2. From the Start menu, right-click My Computer, and select Properties.

3. In System Properties, in the Computer Name tab, write down the following information:

Full Computer Name:_____

Workgroup:_____

MORE INFO   If your computer were a member of a domain, the Full Computer Name field would contain a Domain Name System fully qualified domain name (DNS FQDN), and Workgroup would be replaced with the name of the domain. For example, if you were a member of the contoso.com domain, your full computer name would be computerxx.contoso.com (where computerxx is the name of your computer), and your domain (which would replace the workgroup) would be contoso.com.

4. From the Start menu, select Run. In the Run dialog box, type **cmd** and press ENTER.

5. At the command prompt, type **net config workstation** and press ENTER. An example of the results is shown below.

6. Observe what is displayed in the Command Prompt window and compare it to what is displayed in the Computer Name tab of the System Properties dialog box.

7. Close System Properties. Leave the Command Prompt window open for the next exercise.

EXERCISE 1.4: TAKING A SCREEN SHOT

Estimated completion time: 10 minutes
In the following steps, you will learn to take both a full and active-window screen shot.

1. Press the PRINT SCREEN key (which is sometimes abbreviated as PRTSCN or PRNTSCRN).

2. From the Start menu, select All Programs, Accessories, and then select Paint.

3. In Microsoft Paint, from the Edit menu, select Paste. Observe what is pasted into the current document. Close Microsoft Paint, and do not save changes.

4. Ensure that the Command Prompt window from the previous exercise is active by clicking on the title bar.

5. Press ALT + PRINT SCREEN.

6. From the Start menu, select All Programs, Accessories, and then select WordPad.

7. Press CTRL + V, and observe what is pasted into the current document.

8. Close WordPad and do not save changes.

9. Close the Command Prompt window.

QUESTION What is the difference between the first and second methods of taking a screen shot?

EXERCISE 1.5: COPYING THE LAB MANUAL FOLDER TO SHARED DOCUMENTS

Estimated completion time: 5 minutes

In the following steps, you will copy files needed for this and subsequent labs to Shared Documents.

1. Log on with your administrator account (the password is P@ssw0rd).

2. Insert your Student CD-ROM in the CD-ROM drive.

3. In the D:\ window (the D:\ will be different if your CD-ROM drive is represented by a different letter), select the Lab Manual folder and press CTRL + C.

4. From the Start menu, select My Computer.

5. In My Computer, open Shared Documents.

6. In Shared Documents, press CTRL + V to paste the Lab Manual folder and its contents.

7. Close all open windows.

EXERCISE 1.6: CREATING A TEST USER ACCOUNT

Estimated completion time: 5 minutes

In the following steps, you will create a user account for testing purposes, so that you won't adversely affect other accounts.

1. Log on with your administrator account (the password is P@ssw0rd).

2. From the Start menu, right-click My Computer, and select Manage.

3. In the Computer Management console, in the console tree, expand System Tools, expand Local Users And Groups, and select Users.

4. From the Action menu, select New User.

5. In the New User dialog box, in the User Name text box, type **Test**.

6. Clear the User Must Change Password At Next Logon check box, as shown below. Click Create. Click Close.

7. Close the Computer Management console.

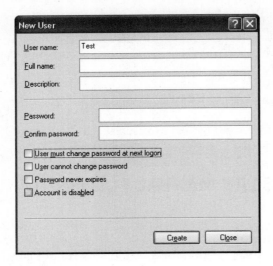

LAB REVIEW QUESTIONS

Estimated completion time: 10 minutes

1. When running the Net Config Workstation command in this lab, was the information displayed about the physical or logical topology of the network?

2. When taking a screen shot, what does pressing the ALT key accomplish?

3. Why, in the interest of security, was it a good idea to demote your student account to User level?

LAB CHALLENGE: ASSIGNING TASKS IN A TECHNICAL SUPPORT ENVIRONMENT

Estimated completion time: 15 minutes

You are a technical support administrator at Proseware, Inc., which supports users of video games. You have been asked to divide support into three categories: Help Desk, Administrator, and Engineer. You have been told that the Help Desk will handle questions concerning configuration issues within the game. Administrators will handle configuration problems that the Help Desk fails to solve, in addition to all operating system and hardware issues. The Engineer group will handle any server-side technical problems that occur for online video games. Assign each group to the appropriate tier and list two to five incidents they might have to handle.

LAB 2
RESOLVING SERVICE CALLS

This lab contains the following exercises and activities:

- Exercise 2.1: Role-Playing: Troubleshooting a Printing Problem

- Exercise 2.2: Role-Playing: Troubleshooting a Graphics Problem

- Exercise 2.3: Finding Solutions at the Microsoft Knowledge Base

- Exercise 2.4: Finding Solutions at Microsoft TechNet

- Lab Review Questions

- Lab Challenge: Creating a Technical Support Documentation Form

SCENARIO

You are a technical support agent for Litware, Inc., which offers technical support for Microsoft products to small companies and residences. It is your job to assist clients with operating system and applications problems.

In this lab you will take turns role-playing a technical support agent and a client. The purpose is to improve your understanding of what is involved in interacting with a client in a technical support environment.

This lab asks you to use some tools not covered in the text and with which you might not be familiar. Don't worry, because the purpose is not to learn the tools, but rather to learn how to interact with a client when you are a technical support agent. The tools are used only as a device to instruct on support–client interaction.

After completing this lab, you will be able to:

- Better understand the roles of technical support agents and clients.

- Use Help and Support and troubleshooters.

- Use the Microsoft Knowledge Base.

- Use Microsoft TechNet.

Estimated lesson time: 80 minutes

EXERCISE 2.1: ROLE-PLAYING: TROUBLESHOOTING A PRINTING PROBLEM

Estimated completion time: 25 minutes

A client calls and explains she has a problem with printing. It is your job to take notes on the issue and resolve it over the phone.

In the following exercise, the student with the lower numbered computer will role-play the client, and the student with the higher numbered computer will role-play technical support.

Creating the Problem

The client should complete the following steps. These steps create the problem that technical support is going to solve. Technical support should not read these steps, and should instead open Notepad and prepare to take notes on the incident (*incident* is a term commonly used in technical support to refer to the interaction between technical support and a client).

1. Log on with your administrator account (the password is P@ssw0rd).

2. From the Start menu, select Printers And Faxes.

3. In the Printers And Faxes window, under the Printer Tasks section on the left, click Add A Printer.

4. In the Add Printer Wizard, on the Welcome page, click Next.

5. On the Local Or Network Printer page, select Local Printer Attached To This Computer, and clear the Automatically Detect And Install My Plug And Play Printer check box. Click Next.

6. On the Select A Printer Port page, select Use The Following Port and, in the drop-down list, select FILE: (Print To File), as seen below. Click Next.

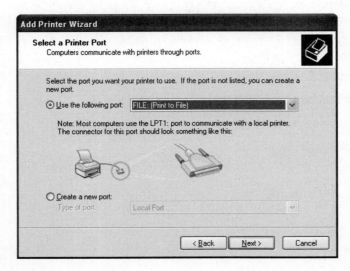

7. On the Install Printer Software page, in the Manufacturer list box, select HP. In the Printers list box, select HP LaserJet 2100. Click Next.

8. On the Name Your Printer page, in the Printer Name text box, verify that HP LaserJet 2100 is entered. Click Next.

9. On the Print Test Page page, under Do You Want To Print A Test Page, select No, and click Next.

10. On the Completing The Add Printer Wizard page, click Finish.

11. Close the Printers And Faxes window.

12. From the Start menu, select My Computer. Browse to Shared Documents\Lab Manual\Lab 2, and open the PrintingProblem document.

> **NOTE**   This file contains a description of the printing problem you are facing as a client and the answers that you will give to questions asked by technical support in the next task. Feel free to improvise answers where information is incomplete. Remember in answering questions that you are playing the role of a naive computer user.

Asking Questions

This task begins the first role-playing scenario. The following questions are to be asked by technical support of the client. The client will be answering the questions according to the PrintingProblem document opened earlier in this lab. All relevant information should be documented in Notepad by the student role-playing technical support.

The following questions are just recommendations and are not comprehensive. Technical support should ask all questions necessary to understand the problem fully.

1. What is the problem?

2. When do you have the problem?

3. Has this problem always occurred?

4. Have you done anything to try to fix the problem yourself?

Re-Creating the Problem

To understand the problem fully, technical support has asked the client to reproduce the problem and describe the steps as he completes them. Therefore, the client will complete the following steps, describing what is happening at each step to technical support.

1. Log on with your student account.

2. From the Start menu, select Run.

3. In the Run dialog box, in the Open text box, type **cmd** and press ENTER.

4. At the command prompt, type **edit**, and press ENTER.

5. In the Edit window, type **Here is some text**.

6. From the File menu, select Print. In the Print Dialog box, verify that Complete Document is selected, and click OK.

7. Wait for a minute for Edit to print to file. It fails with the Edit program appearing as below.

8. Right-click the taskbar and select Task Manager.

9. In Windows Task Manager, in the Applications tab, select C:\Windows\System32\Cmd.exe and click End Task.

10. In the End Program message box, click End Now.

11. Close Windows Task Manager.

Using Help And Support to Find a Solution

The printing problem, as might now be clear, is that the MS-DOS Edit program is trying to print to LPT1, which does not have a printer attached to it. To understand how to use Help And Support to solve this problem, the following steps should be completed by technical support.

1. Log on with your administrator account (the password is P@ssw0rd).

2. From the Start menu, select Help And Support.

3. In the Help And Support Center window, under Pick A Help Topic, click Fixing A Problem.

4. On the Fixing A Problem page, under Fixing A Problem, select Printing Problems, as shown below.

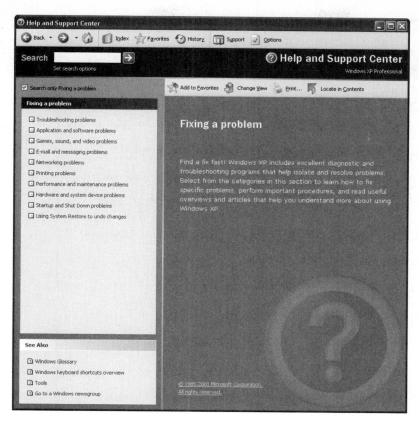

5. On the Printing Problems page, select Printing Troubleshooter.

6. On the Printing Troubleshooter page, select I Can't Print From An MS-DOS-Based Program Or From The MS-DOS Command Line. Clear the I Want The Troubleshooter To Investigate Settings On This Computer check box. Click Next.

7. On the Do You Need To Close The Program From Which You Are Trying To Print page, select No, I Still Cannot Print, and click Next.

8. The Are You Trying To Print To A Shared Printer page appears. Read this page carefully.

   QUESTION This page of the Help And Support Center window suggests that if the printer were shared, you could redirect the output to LPT1 to the shared printer. How can you take advantage of this?

9. On the Are You Trying To Print To A Shared Printer page, expand the To Use The Net.exe Command node. Directions on how to use Net.exe to redirect output from LPT1 to a shared printer appear, as shown on the next page.

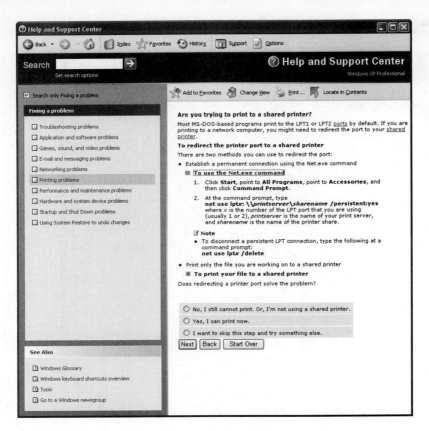

10. Leave the Help And Support Center window open for the next task.

Implementing the Solution

The solution has two steps: First, share the HP printer and, second, follow the Help And Support Center directions on using Net.exe to redirect the LPT1 output to the newly shared HP printer.

The following steps are to be performed by the client, but only according to the instruction of technical support. The client should not read these steps, and should resist the temptation to use skills or knowledge that a naive computer user would not have.

1. Log on with your administrator account (the password is P@ssw0rd).

2. From the Start menu, select Printers And Faxes.

3. In the Printers And Faxes window, right-click HP LaserJet 2100, and select Properties.

4. In the LaserJet 2100 Properties dialog box, in the Sharing tab, click If You Understand The Security Risks But Want To Share Printers Without Running The Wizard, Click Here.

5. In the Enable Printer Sharing message box, select Just Enable Printer Sharing and click OK.

6. In the HP LaserJet 2100 Properties, in the Sharing tab, select Share This Printer. In the Share Name box, type **HP-2100-*xx*** (where *xx* is the number of the client's, or lower numbered, computer). An example is shown below. Click OK.

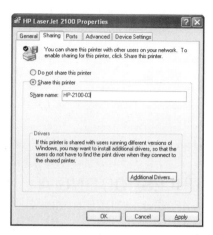

7. Use the instructions in the Help And Support Center window about Net.exe to instruct your client to redirect the output from LPT1 to the shared printer. An example of how this is done is shown below.

8. Close all open windows.

Testing the Solution

The client should complete the following steps. These steps verify that the solution works.

1. From the Start menu, select Run. In the Run dialog box, in the Open text box, type **cmd** and press ENTER.

2. At the command prompt, type **edit** and press ENTER.

3. In the Edit window, type **Here is some text**.

4. From the File menu, select Print.

5. In the Print Dialog Box, click OK. A Print To File dialog box appears.

6. In the Output To File box, type **C:\documents and settings\ administrator\desktop\output.prn,** as seen below, and press ENTER.

7. In the Edit window, from the File menu, select Exit.

8. In the Save File dialog box, click No.

9. At the command prompt, type **exit** and press ENTER.

10. Verify that the Output.prn file is on the desktop, and then delete it.

EXERCISE 2.2: ROLE-PLAYING: TROUBLESHOOTING A GRAPHICS PROBLEM

Estimated completion time: 25 minutes

You are a technical support agent for Litware, Inc. A client has just purchased the popular video game Fruit Stand 3D and receives an error claiming his new, cutting-edge video card does not support Microsoft DirectX 9.0. He knows this to be untrue according to the manufacturer's specifications.

In the following exercise, the student with the higher numbered computer will role-play the client, and the student with the lower numbered computer will role-play technical support.

Creating the DirectX Problem

The client should complete the following steps. These steps create the problem that technical support is going to solve. Technical support should pay no attention to these steps and should instead open Notepad and prepare to take notes on the incident.

Installing DirectX 9.0b

These steps are not necessary if the computer is already running DirectX 9.0b or later. To determine this, run dxdiag from the Run dialog box. The version number of DirectX will appear in the DirectX Diagnostic Tool window in the System tab.

If the graphics card in your computer will not support DirectX 9.0b, you should still role-play the incident as if it could.

1. Log on with your administrator account (the password is P@ssw0rd).

2. From the Start menu, select Internet Explorer.

3. In Microsoft Internet Explorer, in the Address text box, type **http:// www.microsoft.com**.

4. On the Microsoft home page, under the Resources section, click Downloads.

5. On the Download Center page, in the Download Categories section, click DirectX.

6. On the DirectX page, under Most Popular Downloads, click DirectX 9.0b End-User Runtime, as seen below.

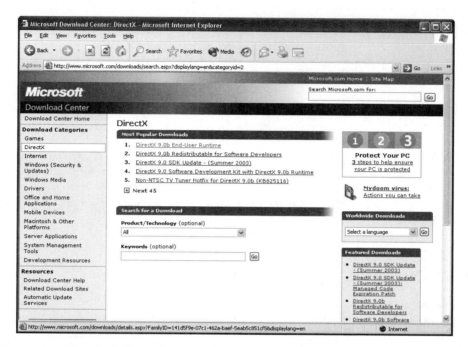

7. On the DirectX 9.0b End-User Runtime page, click Download.

8. In the File Download dialog box, click Open.

9. In the Installing Microsoft(R) DirectX(R) wizard, select I Accept The Agreement, and click Next.

10. On the DirectX Setup page, click Next.

11. The Progress page appears, as shown below. This step might take a few minutes depending on the speed of your Internet connection.

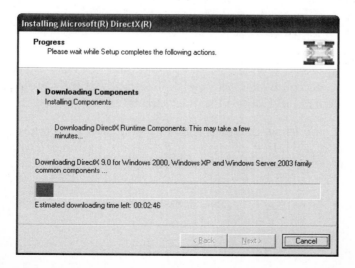

12. On the Restart Computer page of the Installing Microsoft(R) DirectX(R) wizard, click Finish. Your computer will restart.

Breaking DirectX

In the following task, you will cause some components of DirectX to fail.

1. From the Start menu, select My Computer.

2. In My Computer, browse to C:\Windows\System32. You will have to click Show The Contents Of This Folder when appropriate.

3. Locate the file D3d9.dll. Right-click it and select Rename. Rename the file Old_d3d9.dll.

4. Browse to the Shared Documents\Lab Manual\Lab 2 folder and open the DirectXProblem document.

   NOTE   This file contains a description of the DirectX problem you are facing as a client and the answers that you will give to questions asked by technical support in the next task. Feel free to improvise answers where information is incomplete. Remember in answering questions that you are playing the role of a naive computer user.

Asking Questions

The following questions are to be asked by technical support of the client. The client will be answering the questions according to the DirectXProblem text document opened earlier in this lab. All relevant information should be documented in Notepad by the student role-playing technical support.

The following questions are just recommendations and not comprehensive. Technical support should ask all questions necessary to understand the problem fully.

1. What is the problem?

2. When do you have the problem?

3. Has this problem always occurred?

4. Have you done anything to try to fix the problem yourself?

Testing the Problem with Dxdiag.exe

The following steps are to be completed on the client computer at the instruction of technical support. Only technical support should read these steps.

1. As technical support, you know that the problem is probably related to the DirectX installation. Therefore, the following steps use dxdiag.exe to diagnose the problem. Log on with your administrator account (the password is P@ssw0rd).

2. From the Start menu, select Run.

3. In the Run dialog box, in the Open text box, type **dxdiag** and press ENTER.

4. Wait a few moments while the DirectX Diagnostic Tool gathers information.

5. In the DirectX Diagnostic Tool window, in the Display tab, in the DirectX Features section, click Test Direct3D as shown below.

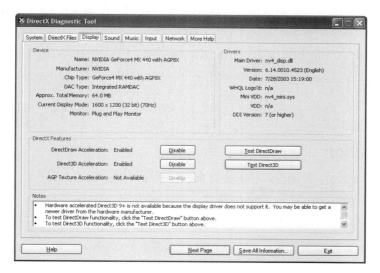

6. In the DirectX Diagnostic Tool message box, in response to the This Will Test Direct3D On This Device, Okay To Proceed question, click Yes.

7. In the DirectX Diagnostic Tool message box, click OK in response to This Test Will Use Hardware Accelerated Direct3D 7 Interfaces.

8. A 3D graphics test will display on your screen. In the DirectX Diagnostic Tool message box, click Yes in response to the Did You See A Spinning Cube With The DirectX Logo On The Sides question.

9. In the DirectX Diagnostic Tool message box, click OK in response to This Test Will Use Hardware Accelerated Direct3D 8 Interfaces.

10. A 3D graphics test will display on your screen. In the DirectX Diagnostic Tool message box, click Yes in response to the Did You See A Spinning Cube With The DirectX Logo On The Sides question.

11. In the DirectX Diagnostic Tool message box, you will see a message that the Direct3D 9 test was skipped because the display driver does not support Direct3D 9. Click OK.

12. In the DirectX Diagnostic Tool window, select the DirectX Files tab.

QUESTION   What is reported in the Notes section?

13. Close the DirectX Diagnostic Tool.

Implementing the Solution

The following task is to be performed on the client computer at the instruction of technical support. The DirectX problem seems to be caused by a missing DLL file, and the DirectX Diagnostic Tool recommends that DirectX be reinstalled. As technical support, you need to lead the client through reinstallation according to the following steps.

1. Log on with your administrator account (the password is P@ssw0rd).

2. Follow the steps outlined in the section "Installing DirectX 9.0b" earlier in this exercise.

Testing the Solution

To test the solution, technical support should instruct the client according to the following steps.

1. Log on with your administrator account (the password is P@ssw0rd).

2. Follow the steps outlined in the section "Testing the Problem with Dxdiag.exe" earlier in this exercise.

EXERCISE 2.3: FINDING SOLUTIONS AT THE MICROSOFT KNOWLEDGE BASE

Estimated completion time: 10 minutes

You are a technical support agent for Litware, Inc. A client is having trouble sending e-mail with Microsoft Outlook 2000. You cannot find help on the issue using the Help in Outlook, so you decide to see if there are any solutions at the Microsoft Knowledge Base.

The following steps should be completed individually. Many of these steps are dependent on the Microsoft Web site. It is possible that the site will have changed since the writing of this exercise. However, the point of the exercise is to navigate to a particular Knowledge Base article, which is possible even if these steps do not match exactly.

1. A client sends you the following e-mail using an Internet e-mail account:

   I am unable to send messages from Microsoft Outlook 2000. My e-mails come back with the following message:

   Your message did not reach some or all of the intended recipients.
   Subject: Test
   Sent: 6/27/2003 11:25 AM
   The following recipient(s) could not be reached:
   John Doe on 6/27/2003 11:25 AM

A syntax error was detected in the content of the message
The MTS-ID of the original message is: c=US;a= ;l=Server-
020127192459Z-145206
MSEXCH:MSExchangeMTA:Site:Server

2. Log on with your student account.

3. From the Start menu, select Internet Explorer.

4. In the Internet Explorer window, in the Address box, type **http://www.microsoft.com** and press ENTER.

5. On the Microsoft home page, in the Resources section, point to Support and then select Knowledge Base.

6. On the Search The Knowledge Base page, in the Select A Microsoft Product drop-down list, select Outlook 2000.

7. In the Search For text box, type **Your message did not reach some or all of the intended recipients**.

8. In the Using drop-down list, select The Exact Phrase Entered, as shown below. Click Go.

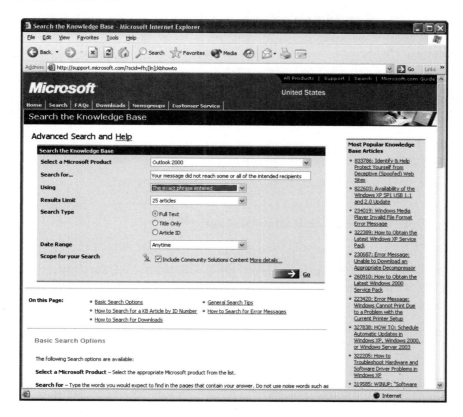

QUESTION How many articles were found using these search criteria?

9. Click the Back button.

10. In the Search For box, type **A syntax error was detected in the content of the message**. Click Go.

11. On the Support And Troubleshooting page, under Search Results, select OL2000: You Receive A Non-Delivery Report When Outlook 2000 Improperly Formats MDBEF Encoding.

> **QUESTION**   According to this article, what could be the solution to your client's e-mail problem?

EXERCISE 2.4: FINDING SOLUTIONS AT MICROSOFT TECHNET

Estimated completion time: 10 minutes

Litware, Inc., would like to save on transportation costs by using Remote Assistance, rather than always driving to remote client sites. Your boss asks you to see if his favorite Microsoft column, Professor Windows, has an article on Remote Assistance.

The following steps should be completed individually. Many of these steps are dependent on the Microsoft Web sites. It is possible that the sites will have changed since the writing of this exercise. However, the point of the exercise is to navigate to a particular TechNet Professor Windows article, which is possible even if these steps do not match the required steps exactly.

1. Log on with your student account.

2. From the Start menu, select Internet Explorer.

3. In the Internet Explorer window, in the Address box, type **http://search.microsoft.com** and press ENTER.

4. On the Search Microsoft.com page, click Advanced Search.

5. Under Microsoft.com Advanced Search, in the All Of These Words box, type **Remote Assistance Professor Windows**.

6. In the Choose A Microsoft.com Site drop-down list, select TechNet. Click Go.

7. On the Search Results From TechNet page, select Windows XP Remote Assistance: Professor Windows, October 2002.

> **QUESTION**   According to the article, what type of encryption is used by Remote Assistance?

> **QUESTION**   What Knowledge Base article that describes the Remote Assistance connection process is referenced?

LAB REVIEW QUESTIONS

Estimated completion time: 10 minutes

1. What did the role-playing exercises demonstrate about offering technical support?

2. What resource built into Microsoft Windows XP offers help for many operating system and application issues, and how can it be accessed?

3. What Microsoft online resources offer comprehensive help on applications, operating systems, and how to plan, deploy, and maintain them?

4. What is the Uniform Resource Locator (URL) for Microsoft TechNet?

5. What application is useful for diagnosing DirectX problems?

6. What type of resource within Help And Support was used to solve the printing problem in Exercise 2.1, and how can it be accessed?

LAB CHALLENGE: CREATING A TECHNICAL SUPPORT DOCUMENTATION FORM

Estimated completion time: 25 minutes

You are a technical support manager for Litware, Inc., a company that offers technical support to users of Microsoft products. When clients call in, you have an application that assists in documenting incidents. However, incidents often are handled at the client's site and you do not have access to that application. You therefore need to create a form for documenting incidents when you are troubleshooting at clients' sites. It can be written in Notepad and should include headings for all pertinent information. After the form is complete, you should fill it out according to the role-playing exercise in which you played technical support.

LAB 3

SIMPLE MICROSOFT WINDOWS XP CONFIGURATION ISSUES

This lab contains the following exercises and activities:

- Exercise 3.1: Configuring the Notification Area
- Exercise 3.2: Configuring Startup Applications
- Exercise 3.3: Configuring Quick Launch
- Exercise 3.4: Configuring the Taskbar
- Exercise 3.5: Configuring the Start Menu
- Exercise 3.6: Configuring Input Languages
- Exercise 3.7: Configuring Folder Settings
- Exercise 3.8: Changing File Associations
- Exercise 3.9: Using Disk Maintenance Utilities
- Lab Review Questions
- Lab Challenge: Creating a Custom Desktop

SCENARIO

You are a Tier 1 technical support agent working at Woodgrove Bank. Woodgrove Bank is a medium-sized company with Microsoft Windows XP workstations attached to a Microsoft Windows Server 2003 Active Directory directory service domain. It is your job to assist employees of Woodgrove Bank with computer-related issues. Throughout this lab, you will be asked to perform simple tasks associated with configuring Windows XP. These tasks are representative of many common tasks that in-house technical support employees deal with regularly.

After completing this lab, you will be able to:

- Configure the notification area
- Configure Startup applications
- Configure Quick Launch
- Configure the taskbar

- Configure the Start menu
- Configure input languages
- Configure folder settings
- Change file associations

Estimated lesson time: 90 minutes

EXERCISE 3.1: CONFIGURING THE NOTIFICATION AREA

Estimated completion time: 5 minutes

Modifying Icon Behavior in the Notification Area

In the following exercise, you will change how icons are displayed in the notification area.

1. Log on with your Test account.

2. Right-click the taskbar and select Task Manager.

3. Observe the CPU Usage icon that appears in the notification area, as shown below.

4. Right-click the taskbar and select Properties.

5. In the Taskbar And Start Menu Properties, in the Notification Area section, click Customize.

6. In the Customize Notifications dialog box, select CPU Usage in the Current Items list box, and select Always Hide in the drop-down list, as shown below.

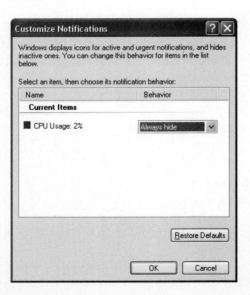

7. In the Taskbar And Start Menu Properties, click OK.

8. Notice that the Task Manager icon is no longer visible in the notification area.

9. Close the Windows Task Manager.

> **QUESTION**   Without changing any settings, how can you view the CPU Usage icon in the notification area?

Restoring the Notification Area Defaults

1. Right-click the taskbar and select Properties.

2. In the Taskbar And Start Menu Properties, in the Notification Area section, click Customize.

3. In the Customize Notifications dialog box, click Restore Defaults, and click OK.

4. In the Taskbar And Start Menu Properties, click OK.

EXERCISE 3.2: CONFIGURING STARTUP APPLICATIONS

Estimated completion time: 15 minutes

In the following exercise, you will create and configure startup applications.

1. Log on with your administrator account (the password is P@ssw0rd).

2. From the Start menu, choose All Programs, right-click Startup, and select Open All Users.

3. In the Startup folder, from the File menu, point to New, and then select Text Document. Open New Text Document.

4. In the New Text Document – Notepad window, type the following:

Notepad C:\Documents and Settings\All Users\documents\helloworld.txt

5. From the File menu, select Save As.

6. In the Save As dialog box, in the File Name box, type **test.bat** and click Save.

7. From the File menu, select Exit.

8. In the Startup folder, select New Text Document and press DELETE. Click Yes to confirm that you want to delete the file.

9. In the Address box of the Startup folder, type: **C:\Documents and Settings\All Users\Documents** and press ENTER.

10. In the Shared Documents folder, from the File menu, point to New, and then select Text Document. Type **Helloworld** for the name, and press ENTER.

11. Open the Helloworld text document.

12. In the Helloworld – Notepad window, type **Hello World!**

13. From the File menu, select Save. Close the Helloworld – Notepad window.

14. Log off, and log back on with your student account.

> **QUESTION**   What happens when you log on?

15. Close any open windows and log off. Log back on with your administrator account. Once logged on, close any open windows.

16. From the Start menu, select Run.

17. In the Run dialog box, in the Open text box, type **msconfig** and press ENTER.

18. In the System Configuration Utility, in the Startup tab, in the Startup Item column, clear the Test check box, as shown below, and click OK.

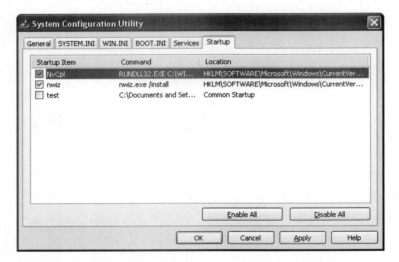

19. In the System Configuration message box, click Restart.

20. After your computer has rebooted, log on with your administrator account.

21. In the System Configuration Utility dialog box, select the Don't Show This Message Or Launch The System Configuration Utility When Windows Starts check box and click OK.

22. From the Start menu, point to All Programs, right-click Startup, and select Open All Users.

23. Close the Startup Folder.

> **QUESTION**   What happened to the Test.bat file that you created in this folder?

EXERCISE 3.3: CONFIGURING QUICK LAUNCH

Estimated completion time: 10 minutes

The head of a division at Woodgrove Bank often audits a database file stored on a network share. He dislikes having to browse over the network to the file, and likes to keep his desktop free from shortcuts. He wants to be able to open the file the same way he opens Microsoft Excel, which is from Quick Launch.

> **NOTE** You will need a partner for this exercise. Both students are to complete the following steps.

1. Log on with your student account.

2. Right-click the taskbar, and select Properties.

3. In the Taskbar And Start Menu Properties, in the Taskbar tab, in the Taskbar Appearance section, select the Show Quick Launch check box and click OK.

4. Log off and log back on with your administrator account.

5. From the Start menu, select My Computer, and open Shared Documents.

6. In the Shared Documents folder, from the File menu, select New, and then select Folder. For the folder name, type **Share** and press ENTER.

7. Right-click the Share folder and select Properties.

8. In the Share Properties, in the Sharing tab, in the Network Sharing And Security section, select the Share This Folder On The Network check box. Also select the Allow Network Users To Change My Files check box. Click OK.

> **NOTE** Before completing step 8, you might need to click If You Understand The Security Risks But Want To Share Files Without Running The Wizard, Click Here, and in the subsequent Enable File Sharing message box, select Just Enable File Sharing and click OK.

9. In the Shared Documents folder, open the Share folder.

10. In the Share folder, from the File menu, select New, and select Text Document. For the name, type **Database File**, and press ENTER.

> **NOTE** Wait until your partner has finished steps 1 through 10 before continuing.

11. Log off and log back on with your student account.

12. From the Start menu, select Run. In the Run dialog box, in the Open text box, type **Computerxx** (where **Computerxx** is the name of your partner's computer) and click OK.

13. In the Computerxx window, open the Share folder. In the Share On Computerxx folder, drag the Database File text document to Quick Launch using the left mouse button, as seen below.

14. From Quick Launch, click the text document icon.

> **QUESTION** What happens when you click the text document icon?

EXERCISE 3.4: CONFIGURING THE TASKBAR

Estimated completion time: 10 minutes

An employee at Woodgrove Bank complains that her taskbar is "always there," "always in the way," that it "groups things together," and that she "cannot resize or move it."

You need to reconfigure her taskbar so that it is hidden when not in use, can be behind windows, does not group similar taskbar buttons, and is not locked.

1. Log on with your Test account.

2. Right-click the taskbar and select Properties.

3. In the Taskbar And Start Menu Properties, clear the Lock The Taskbar, Group Similar Taskbar Buttons, and Keep The Taskbar On Top Of Other Windows check boxes.

4. Select the Auto-Hide The Taskbar check box. An example of the new settings is shown below. Click OK.

5. After observing the effects of these changes, return your Test taskbar to its original state.

Adding a Desktop Toolbar to the Taskbar

A user who has a lot of desktop shortcuts complains that he cannot access them easily when he has windows open. You need to set his system up so that he can access everything on his desktop from the taskbar. He would also like to be able to access his favorite links in Microsoft Internet Explorer from the taskbar. Finally, he wants to be able to access a network share from the taskbar.

1. Right-click the taskbar, point to Toolbars, and select Desktop.

2. Click the Desktop button on the taskbar to observe what it contains, as shown below.

Adding a Favorites Toolbar to the Taskbar

1. Right-click the taskbar, select Toolbars, and select Links.

2. From the Start menu, select Internet Explorer.

3. In the Internet Explorer window, in the Address box, type **http:// www.microsoft.com** and press ENTER.

4. From the Favorites menu, select Add To Favorites.

5. In the Add Favorite dialog box, ensure that Microsoft Corporation is in the Name text box, and click OK. Close Internet Explorer.

6. Click the Links button in the taskbar.

   QUESTION   Why doesn't the link to Microsoft Corporation appear?

7. Right-click the taskbar, point to Toolbars, and select New Toolbar.

8. In the New Toolbar dialog box, in the Folder text box, type **C:\Documents and Settings\Test\favorites**. Click OK.

9. Right-click the taskbar, point to Toolbars, and deselect Links.

10. In the taskbar, click the Favorites button, and observe that the link to Microsoft Corporation is present, as seen below.

Adding a Network Share Toolbar to the Taskbar

1. Right-click the taskbar, point to Toolbars, and then select New Toolbar.

2. In the New Toolbar dialog box, in the Folder text box, type **\\computer.xx\ share** (where **computer.xx** is the name of your partner's computer).

EXERCISE 3.5: CONFIGURING THE START MENU

Estimated completion time: 15 minutes

You want a new program group called Woodgrove Bank to appear in the Start menu under All Programs for all users of a computer. This entry should be the first program group listed, before Accessories. You also want to move the Windows Update shortcut from All Programs to the Start menu. Finally, you want a shortcut to the Network Connections Folder and Administrative Tools to appear in the Start menu for easy access for the Administrator account.

Adding the Woodgrove Bank Program Group to All Programs

The following steps will add a new program group to All Programs.

1. Log on with your administrator account (the password is P@ssw0rd).

2. From the Start menu, select My Computer and, in the My Computer window, navigate to the folder C:\Documents and Settings\All Users\Start Menu\Programs.

   NOTE   Another way to access the All Users\Start Menu\Programs folder is to right-click the Start button and select Open All Users or Explore All Users and then double-click the Programs folder.

3. In the Programs folder, from the File menu, point to New and then select Folder. For the folder name, type **Woodgrove Bank** and press ENTER.

   QUESTION   Why does the icon for the Woodgrove Bank folder differ from an ordinary folder?

4. Close the Programs folder.

5. From the Start Menu, select All Programs.

6. Find the Woodgrove Bank program group and drag it with the left mouse button so that the location bar is above Accessories, and then release the left mouse button. The result is shown below.

Moving the Windows Update Shortcut from All Programs to the Start Menu

In the following steps, you will incorrectly move the Windows Update Shortcut, and then fix the error.

1. From the Start menu, select All Programs, and then right-click Windows Update. Select Pin To Start Menu.

2. In the All Programs menu, right-click Windows Update and select Delete. Click Yes to confirm that you want to delete the Windows Update shortcut from the All Programs menu.

3. Log off and log back on with your administrator account.

4. From the Start menu, right-click Windows Update, and select Properties.

   QUESTION   Make an educated guess about why the Windows Update shortcut in the Start menu is configured incorrectly.

5. Close the Windows Update Properties.

6. Right-click the Start button and select Open All Users.

7. In the Create Shortcut wizard, in the Type The Location Of The Item text box, type **%SystemRoot%\system32\wupdmgr.exe**, and click Next.

8. In the Select A Title For The Program dialog box, in the Type A Name For This Shortcut box, type **Windows Update** and click Finish.

9. From the Start menu, right-click Windows Update and select Properties. The Properties dialog box is shown below.

   IMPORTANT   The shortcut has reestablished its relationship with the shortcut for Windows Update in All Programs, and will work correctly again.

10. Close all open windows.

Adding the Network Connections Folder and Administrative Tools to the Start Menu

In the following steps, you will learn to add shortcuts to useful administrative locations to the Start menu.

1. Right-click the Start menu and select Properties.

2. In the Taskbar And Start Menu Properties, in the Start Menu tab, click Customize.

3. In the Customize Start Menu dialog box, in the Advanced tab, in the Start Menu Items list box, locate Network Connections and select Link To Network Connections Folder.

4. In the Start Menu Items list box, locate System Administrative Tools and select Display On The All Programs Menu And The Start Menu. Click OK.

5. In the Taskbar And Start Menu Properties, click OK.

6. Verify that these items were successfully added to the Start menu.

> **QUESTION**   Why won't these items also be added to your student account Start menu?

EXERCISE 3.6: CONFIGURING INPUT LANGUAGES

Estimated completion time: 10 minutes
Woodgrove Bank has international business interests and, as such, some of the employees are bilingual. You are sometimes called on to deal with language-related computer issues.

Assigning Russian as the Input Language

A bilingual executive is going to Russia to negotiate with a software development company and would like his computer to use Russian as the input language.

1. Log on with your Test account.

2. From the Start menu, select Control Panel.

3. In the Control Panel window, if the Control Panel is configured to show the Category view, click Switch To Classic View.

4. Double-click Regional And Language Options.

5. In the Regional And Language Options dialog box, in the Languages tab, in the Text Services And Input Languages section, click Details.

6. In the Text Services And Input Languages dialog box, in the Installed Services section, click Add.

7. In the Add Input Languages dialog box, in the Input Language drop-down list, select Russian. Click OK.

8. Verify that the Text Services And Input Languages dialog box appears like the example below, and click OK.

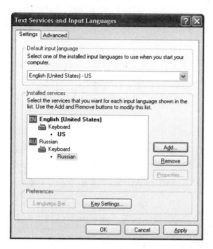

9. In the Regional And Language Options dialog box, click OK.

10. From the Start menu, select All Programs, Accessories, and then select Notepad.

11. In the Untitled – Notepad window, type some random letters. Press the left ALT + SHIFT keys and then type some more random characters. Notice that the input language is toggled.

12. Close all open windows, discarding changes.

Removing the ALT + SHIFT Language Toggle Option

On his return, the executive from the previous task complains that when he is using his word processing program sometimes the input language changes from English to Russian or vice versa. You need to make it so that keystrokes cannot change the input language.

1. From the Start menu, select Control Panel. In Control Panel, double-click Regional And Language Options.

2. In the Regional And Language Options dialog box, in the Languages tab, in the Text Services And Input Languages section, click Details.

3. In the Text Services And Input Languages dialog box, in the Preferences section, click Key Settings.

4. In the Advanced Key Settings dialog box, click Change Key Sequences.

5. In the Change Key Sequence dialog box, clear the Switch Input Languages check box, as shown below, and click OK.

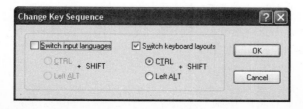

6. In the Advanced Key Settings dialog box, click OK.

7. In the Text Services And Input Languages dialog box, click OK.

8. In the Regional And Language Options dialog box, click OK.

9. Close Control Panel.

EXERCISE 3.7: CONFIGURING FOLDER SETTINGS

Estimated completion time: 5 minutes

An employee at Woodgrove Bank would like her folders to behave differently in several ways. First, she wants each new folder opened to have its own window. Second, she would like her folder to behave more like a Web page, so that she needs to click only once to open an item rather than double-clicking. Third, she wants to be able to see file extensions.

Also, you have recently been warned of a computer virus that spread through Woodgrove Bank that creates a hidden folder called Attack on the root of the C drive. You want to change folder settings so that you can easily see if this folder exists on her C drive.

1. Log on with your Test account.

2. From the Start menu, select Control Panel. If Control Panel is using the Category view, click Switch To Classic View in the left pane.

3. In the Control Panel window, double-click Folder Options.

4. In the Folder Options dialog box, in the General tab, in the Tasks section, select Use Windows Classic Folders.

5. In the Browse Folders section, select Open Each Folder In The Same Window.

6. In the Click Items As Follows section, select Single-Click To Open An Item (Point To Select), as shown below.

7. In the View tab, in the Advanced Settings list box, under Files And Folders, clear the Hide Extensions For Known File Types check box.

8. In the Advanced Settings list box, under Hidden Files And Folders, select Show Hidden Files And Folders. Click OK.

   QUESTION   *Why are the icon titles now underlined?*

9. In Control Panel, click Folder Options and, in the General tab, click Restore Defaults. In the View Tab, click Restore Defaults. Click OK.

10. Close Control Panel.

EXERCISE 3.8: CHANGING FILE ASSOCIATIONS

Estimated completion time: 5 minutes

A user would like the text files he opens to open in WordPad by default, instead of in Notepad.

1. Log on with your administrator account (the password is P@ssw0rd).

2. From the Start menu, select Control Panel. In the Control Panel window, switch to Classic view, and double-click Folder Options.

3. In the Folder Options dialog box, in the File Types tab, in the Registered File Type list box, in the Extensions column, select TXT. In the Details For 'TXT' Extension section, click Change.

4. In the Open With dialog box, under Recommended Programs, select WordPad. Click OK.

5. Browse to the location Shared Documents\Share and open the Database File text document. Note that it opens in WordPad.

6. In Control Panel, select Folder Options. In the Folder Options dialog box, in the File Types tab, in the Registered File Types list, in the Extensions column, select TXT.

7. In the Details For 'TXT' Extension section, select Restore.

8. In the Folder Options dialog box, click Close.

9. Close all open windows.

EXERCISE 3.9: USING DISK MAINTENANCE UTILITIES

Estimated completion time: 5 minutes

A user complains of slow disk performance, and says she received notice of two write errors to her C drive in an application she uses.

In the following steps, you will schedule a disk check and analyze the need to defragment the C drive.

1. Log on with your administrator account (the password is P@ssw0rd).

2. From the Start menu, select My Computer.

3. In My Computer, right-click the Local Disk (C:), and select Properties.

4. In the Local Disk (C:) Properties, in the Tools tab, in the Error-Checking section, click Check Now.

5. In the Check Disk Local Disk (C:) dialog box, select the Automatically Fix File System Errors check box, as seen below, and then click Start.

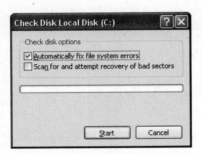

6. In the Checking Disk Local Disk (C:) message box, click Yes to schedule the disk check during the next startup.

7. In the Local Disk (C:) Properties, in the Defragmentation section, click Defragment Now.

8. In the Disk Defragmenter, click Analyze.

9. In the Disk Defragmenter dialog box, click View Report. An example report is shown below.

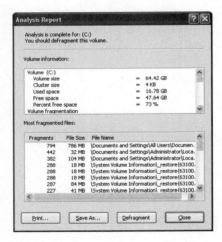

10. Close all open windows and restart your computer.

LAB REVIEW QUESTIONS

Estimated completion time: 15 minutes

1. What is the portion of the taskbar that contains the system clock and other icons called?

2. What utility can you use to easily change which applications run automatically on startup?

3. How can you set an item to start on startup for all users of a computer?

4. Can only applications be configured to launch from Quick Launch?

5. How can you help to minimize the number of taskbar buttons on a taskbar, using taskbar settings?

6. By default, how many frequently used programs appear on the Start menu?

7. What is the default keystroke to toggle between input languages in Windows XP?

8. What item in Control Panel, in Classic view, should you select to alter file associations?

LAB CHALLENGE: CREATING A CUSTOM DESKTOP

Estimated completion time: 25 minutes

Woodgrove Bank is not satisfied with the default settings for the way the Windows desktop behaves. They have asked you to come up with a way to create a custom feel to the desktop for two different departments. You need to make changes in every area covered in this lab to create two custom desktops that are different from each other. One should be targeted toward Power Users and allow more functionality, and the other should be targeted toward call-center employees, and should simplify the desktop to limit distraction.

Be sure to change only the Test account; first implement one custom desktop and then the other. The changes should include modifying the following:

■ Notification area

■ Quick Launch

■ Taskbar

■ Start menu

■ Input languages

■ Folder settings

■ File associations

LAB 4:
MICROSOFT OUTLOOK AND OUTLOOK EXPRESS

This lab contains the following exercises and activities:

- Exercise 4.1: Installing Microsoft Office Outlook 2003
- Exercise 4.2: Configuring Microsoft Outlook as a POP3 Mail Client
- Exercise 4.3: Configuring Microsoft Outlook as an IMAP Mail Client
- Exercise 4.4: Configuring .pst File Locations
- Exercise 4.5: Backing Up Outlook Data
- Exercise 4.6: Common Configuration Options in Outlook
- Exercise 4.7: Configuring a Newsgroup Client in Outlook Express
- Exercise 4.8: Maintaining Outlook
- Lab Review Questions
- Lab Challenge: Configuring Outlook Express as an E-Mail Client

BEFORE YOU BEGIN

If you have not completed "Exercise 3.3: Configuring Quick Launch," you will need to complete the following steps, which will create a shared folder.

1. Log on with your administrator account.
2. From the Start menu, select My Computer, and open Shared Documents.
3. In the Shared Documents folder, from the File menu, select New, and then select Folder. For the folder name, type **Share** and press ENTER.
4. Right-click the Share folder and select Properties.
5. In the Share Properties, in the Sharing tab, in the Network Sharing And Security section, select the Share This Folder On The Network check box. Also select the Allow Network Users To Change My Files check box. Click OK.

    NOTE Before completing step 5, you might need to click If You Understand The Security Risks But Want To Share Files Without Running The Wizard, Click Here, and in the subsequent Enable File Sharing message box, select Just Enable File Sharing and click OK.

SCENARIO

You are a Tier 1 technical support agent at Consolidated Messenger, a courier company serving metropolitan areas across the United States. The company is upgrading to Microsoft Office Outlook 2003 and there are many installation and configuration tasks to complete. Furthermore, the company has started its own news server, and newsreader clients need to be configured.

After completing this lab, you will be able to:

- Install Outlook 2003

- Configure Outlook as a POP3 and IMAP e-mail client

- Configure the location of .pst files

- Back up Outlook data

- Perform common Outlook configuration tasks

- Subscribe to a newsgroup using Outlook Express

- Perform common maintenance tasks in Outlook

- Configure Outlook Express as an e-mail client

Estimated lesson time: 95 minutes

EXERCISE 4.1: INSTALLING MICROSOFT OFFICE OUTLOOK 2003

Estimated completion time: 10 minutes
In the following steps, you will install Outlook 2003.

1. Log on with your administrator account (the password is P@ssw0rd).

2. Insert your Microsoft Office Professional Edition 2003 CD into your CD-ROM drive.

3. In the Microsoft Office 2003 Setup window, on the Product Key page, type your product key and click Next.

4. On the User Information page, click Next.

5. On the End User License Agreement page, select the I Accept The Terms In The License Agreement check box, and click Next.

6. On the Type Of Installation page, select Custom Install, and click Next.

7. On the Custom Setup page, clear all the check boxes except for the Outlook check box, as shown below. Click Next.

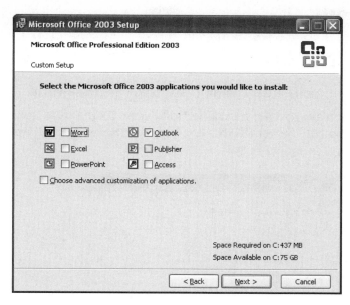

8. On the Summary page, click Install.

9. On the Now Installing Office page, the progress of the installation is displayed.

10. On the Setup Completed page, click Finish.

EXERCISE 4.2: CONFIGURING MICROSOFT OUTLOOK AS A POP3 MAIL CLIENT

Estimated completion time: 10 minutes

Consolidated Messenger recently merged with another company. The new company uses a Post Office Protocol 3 (POP3) e-mail server, whereas Consolidated Messenger uses an Internet Message Access Protocol (IMAP) server. You need to configure Outlook to receive e-mail from both these servers without interference. You want the messages from each to remain in separate data stores when downloaded in Outlook.

In this exercise, you will configure Outlook as a POP3 mail client.

1. Log on with your student account.

2. From the Start menu, select E-Mail.

3. In the Outlook 2003 Startup wizard, click Next.

4. In the Account Configuration wizard, on the E-Mail Accounts Page, verify that Yes is selected, and click Next.

5. In the E-Mail Accounts wizard, on the Server Type page, select POP3, and click Next.

6. On the Internet E-Mail Settings (POP3) page, under User Information, in the Your Name text box, type *your name*. In the E-Mail Address text box, type **studentxx@contoso.com**, where studentxx is your student account user name.

7. Under Logon Information, in the Password text box, type **P@ssw0rd**.

8. Under Server Information, in the Incoming Mail Server (POP3) text box, and in the Outgoing Mail Server (SMTP) text box, type **Server**. An example of theses settings is shown below. Click Next.

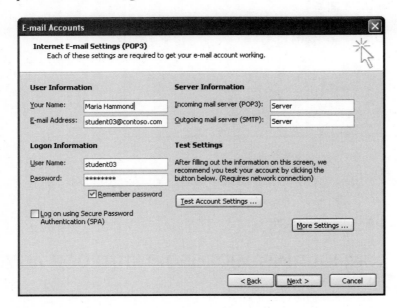

9. On the Congratulations page, click Finish.

10. In the User Name message box, click OK.

11. In the Microsoft Office 2003 Activation Wizard, verify that I Want To Activate The Software Over The Internet is selected, and click Next.

12. In the Microsoft Office 2003 Activation Wizard, click Close.

13. In Microsoft Outlook, click New.

14. In the Untitled – Message window, in the To text box, type **studentxx@contoso.com**, where **studentxx** is your student account user name. In the Subject text box, type **test**. Click Send.

15. In Microsoft Outlook, click Send/Receive. You should receive a message from yourself in the Inbox.

16. Close Outlook.

EXERCISE 4.3: CONFIGURING MICROSOFT OUTLOOK AS AN IMAP MAIL CLIENT

Estimated completion time: 10 minutes

In the following exercise, you will create a separate profile for an IMAP account, and configure Outlook as an IMAP client.

1. Log on with your student account.

2. From the Start menu, select Control Panel.

3. In Control Panel, if Control Panel is in Category view, click Switch To Classic View.

4. Double-click Mail.

5. In the Mail Setup – Outlook dialog box, click Show Profiles.

6. In the Mail dialog box, click Add.

7. In the New Profile dialog box, in the Profile Name text box, type **IMAP** and click OK.

8. In the E-Mail Accounts wizard, in the E-Mail section, verify that Add A New E-Mail Account is selected and click Next.

9. On the Server Type page, select IMAP and click Next.

10. On the Internet E-Mail Settings (IMAP) page, under User Information, in the Your Name text box, type your name. In the E-Mail Address text box, type **student*xx*@contoso.com**, where student*xx* is your student account user name.

11. Under Logon Information, in the Password text box, type **P@ssw0rd**.

12. Under Server Information, in the Incoming Mail Server (IMAP) text box, and in the Outgoing Mail Server (SMTP) text box, type **Server**. Click Next.

13. On the Congratulations page, click Finish.

14. In the Mail dialog box, select Prompt For A Profile To Be Used. Click OK.

15. From the Start menu, select E-Mail.

16. In the Choose Profile dialog box, in the Profile Name drop-down list, select IMAP, as shown below, and click OK.

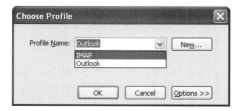

17. In Microsoft Outlook, click New.

18. In the Untitled – Message window, in the To text box, type **student.x.x@ contoso.com**, where student*xx* is your student account user name. In the Subject text box, type **test**. Click Send.

19. In Microsoft Outlook, click Send/Receive. Your test message should appear in Inbox In Server, as shown below.

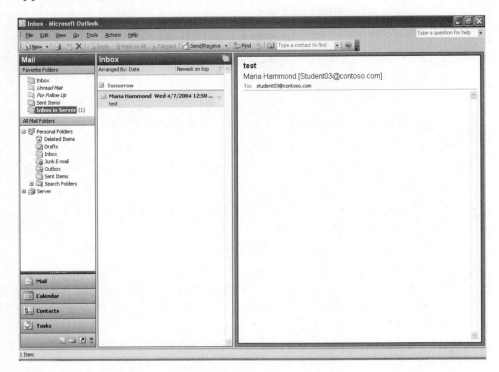

20. Close all open windows.

EXERCISE 4.4: CONFIGURING .PST FILE LOCATIONS

Estimated completion time: 15 minutes

As a technical support agent, you often are away from your computer. You want to be able to check your e-mail on computers that are not yours, after logging on with your administrator account. You need to be able to download e-mail from the server to the same location regardless of the computer you are using on the network.

> **NOTE**   You will need a partner for this exercise.

In the following exercise, you will move the data stores for your e-mail account to a network share, so that they can be accessed from any computer with access to the network. You will then configure Outlook accordingly.

1. Log on with your administrator account (the password is P@ssw0rd).

2. From the Start menu, select Search. In the Search Results window, right-click the animated dog and click Turn Off The Animated Character. Under What Do You Want To Search For, select All Files And Folders.

3. Under Search By Any Or All Of The Criteria Below, in the All Or Part Of The File Name text box, type ***.pst**. In the Look In drop-down list, select Local Disk (C:).

4. Click More Advanced Options. Select the Search Hidden Files And Folders check box. Click Search.

5. Three files appear in the Search Results window, two of which are Outlook and Outlook1, as shown below. Select both of these and, from the Edit menu, select Cut. Close the Search Results window.

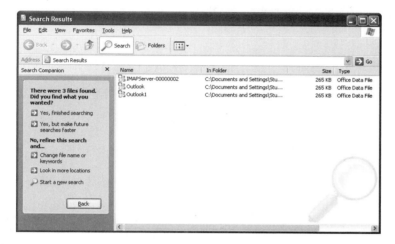

6. From the Start menu, select Run.

7. In the Run dialog box, in the Open text box, type **\\computer.xx**, where computer.xx is the name of your partner's computer.

8. In the Computer.xx window, double-click Share.

9. In the Share On Computer.xx folder, from the File menu, select New and then select Folder. Name the new folder E-Mail Data Files. Open the E-Mail Data Files folder.

10. In the E-Mail Data Files folder, from the Edit menu, select Paste. Close the E-Mail Data Files folder.

QUESTION   Why not also copy the third .pst file to this location?

11. Log off and log back on with your student account.

12. From the Start menu, select E-Mail.

13. In the Choose Profile dialog box, in the Profile Name drop-down list, select IMAP and click OK.

14. In the Personal Folders message box, note what file is missing and click OK.

15. In the Create/Open Personal Folders File dialog box, browse to the E-Mail Data Files folder you created on your partner's computer, and select the missing file, as shown below. Click Open.

16. Close Microsoft Outlook.

17. From the Start menu, select E-Mail.

18. In the Choose Profile dialog box, in the Profile Name drop-down list, select Outlook and click OK.

19. In the Personal Folders message box, note which file is missing and click OK.

20. In the Create/Open Personal Folders File dialog box, browse to the E-Mail Data Files folder you created on your partner's computer, and select the missing file. Click Open.

21. In the Microsoft Outlook Message box, click OK. Outlook automatically closes. The .pst file location is now configured correctly, and Outlook will start normally.

EXERCISE 4.5: BACKING UP OUTLOOK DATA

Estimated completion time: 10 minutes

A user is concerned about her e-mail. She uses her computer almost purely as an e-mail client, which is how she performs the majority of her communication. Although her entire system is backed up weekly, she wants you to show her a method that she can use whenever she wants.

In the following exercise, you will back up Outlook data to a .PST file.

1. Log on with your student account.

2. From the Start menu, select E-Mail.

3. In the Choose Profile dialog box, in the Profile Name drop-down list, select Outlook and then click OK.

4. From the File menu, select Import And Export.

5. In the Import And Export Wizard, in the Choose An Action To Perform list, select Export To A File. Click Next.

6. On the Export To A File page, in the Create A File Of Type list, select Personal Folder File (.pst) and click Next.

7. On the Export Personal Folders page, in the Select The Folder To Export From list, select Personal Folders (the outermost folder), select the Include Subfolders check box, as shown below, and then click Next.

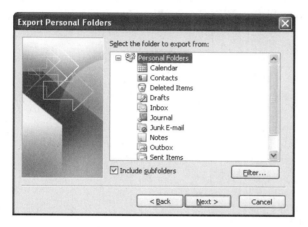

8. On the Export Personal Folders page, click Browse.

9. In the Open Personal Folders dialog box, click the Desktop icon on the left, and click OK.

10. On the Export Personal Folders page, click Finish.

11. In the Create Microsoft Personal Folders dialog box, click OK.

12. Close Outlook and verify that there is a backup file on your desktop.

EXERCISE 4.6: COMMON CONFIGURATION OPTIONS IN OUTLOOK

Estimated completion time: 10 minutes

An employee of Consolidated Messenger has some requests for how he wants Outlook to perform. First, he dislikes that his messages are sent immediately; he would prefer that they be sent when he clicks Send/Receive. Second, he would like to be able to access his e-mail account from his computer at home over the Internet, and be able to view e-mails he has already downloaded at work. Third, he sends e-mails to some people that use old e-mail programs, and would like his e-mails to be maximally compatible. Fourth, in Microsoft Outlook 2000, he would see images in some e-mails, and now, in Outlook 2003, he doesn't; he wants this changed. Finally, he would like tighter restrictions on junk e-mail.

Disable Send Immediately When Connected

In the following steps, you will configure when Outlook sends and receives e-mails.

1. Log on with your student account.

2. From the Start menu, select E-Mail.

3. In the Choose Profile dialog box, in the Profile Name drop-down list, select Outlook and then click OK.

4. In Microsoft Outlook, from the Tools menu, select Options.

5. In the Options dialog box, in the Mail Setup tab, clear the Send Immediately When Connected check box, as shown below.

Enable Leave Messages On Server

In the following steps, you will instruct Outlook to leave a copy of messages on the e-mail server after they have been downloaded.

1. In the Mail Setup tab, click E-Mail Accounts.

2. In the E-Mail Accounts wizard, verify that View Or Change Existing E-Mail Accounts is selected, and then click Next.

3. On the E-Mail Accounts page, click Change.

4. On the Internet E-Mail Settings (POP3) page, click More Settings.

5. In the Internet E-Mail Settings dialog box, in the Advanced tab, select the Leave A Copy Of Messages On The Server check box, as shown below. Click OK.

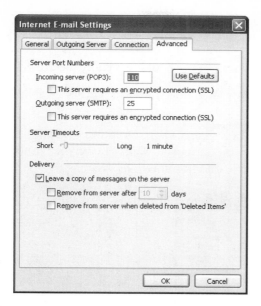

6. In the E-Mail Accounts wizard, on the Internet E-Mail Settings (POP3) page, click Next.

7. On the E-Mail Accounts page, click Cancel.

Using Plaintext to Create Messages

Messages written in plaintext are more compatible with other e-mail programs. The following steps will configure Outlook to create text-only messages.

1. In the Options dialog box, select the Mail Format tab.

2. In the Compose In This Message Format drop-down list, choose Plain Text.

Enable Automatic Download of Images in E-Mails

The following steps will automatically download images in e-mails that a user receives.

1. In the Security tab, click Change Automatic Download Settings.

2. In the Automatic Picture Download Settings dialog box, clear the Don't Download Pictures Or Other Content Automatically In HTML E-Mail check box. Click Cancel.

3. In the Options dialog box, click OK.

Limiting Junk E-Mail

The following steps will help to limit the amount of junk e-mail received.

1. From the Actions menu, select Junk E-Mail and then select Junk E-Mail Options.

2. In the Junk E-Mail Options dialog box, select High: Most Junk E-Mail Is Caught, But Some Regular Mail May Be Caught As Well. Check Your Junk E-Mail Folder Often, as shown below. Click Cancel.

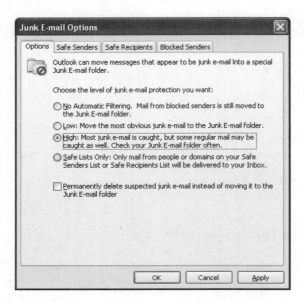

EXERCISE 4.7: CONFIGURING A NEWSGROUP CLIENT IN OUTLOOK EXPRESS

Estimated completion time: 10 minutes

Consolidated Messenger has started a newsgroup to keep employees informed on policies and to create a forum for discussion.

In the following steps, you will configure Outlook Express to subscribe to a newsgroup. You will also post a message to the newsgroup.

1. Log on with your student account.

2. From the Start menu, select All Programs, and then select Outlook Express. When asked if you want to make Outlook Express your default mail client, click No.

3. In the Internet Connection Wizard, on the Your Name page, click Cancel. In the Internet Connection Wizard message box, click Yes.

4. In the Outlook Express Import wizard, click Cancel. In the Import Messages message box, click Yes.

5. From the Tools menu, select Accounts. In the Internet Accounts dialog box, in the All tab, click Add and select News.

6. In the Internet Connection Wizard, on the Your Name page, in the Display Name text box, type your name and then click Next.

7. On the Internet News E-Mail Address page, in the E-Mail Address text box, type **studentxx@contoso.com**, where studentxx is your student account user name. Click Next.

8. On the Internet News Server Name page, in the News (NNTP) Server text box, type **Server**. Select the My News Server Requires Me To Log On check box, and click Next.

9. On the Internet News Server Logon page, in the Account text box, type **studentxx**, where studentxx is your student account user name. In the Password text box type **P@ssw0rd**. Click Next.

10. On the Congratulations page, click Finish.

11. In the Internet Accounts dialog box, click Close. In the Outlook Express message box, click Yes.

12. In the Internet News Subscriptions dialog box, in the All list box, select Classroom and click Subscribe. Click OK.

13. In Outlook Express, in the Folders pane, select Classroom. On the toolbar, click New Post.

14. In the New Message dialog box, in the Subject text box, type **From Studentxx**, where Studentxx is your student account user name. Click Send.

15. In the Post News message box, click OK.

16. From the Tools menu, select Synchronize Newsgroups.

17. In the Synchronize Newsgroup dialog box, select the Get The Following Items check box, and click OK. Messages posted to the newsgroup by other students should arrive.

18. Close Outlook Express.

EXERCISE 4.8: MAINTAINING OUTLOOK

Estimated completion time: 10 minutes

An employee at Consolidated Messenger has a very large store of e-mails and would like to keep the size manageable. You should implement policies that both prevent buildup of deleted e-mails and contract the size of all e-mails.

Emptying Deleted Items Folder on Exiting

The following steps will prevent the buildup of deleted e-mails.

1. Log on with your student account.

2. From the Start menu, select E-Mail.

3. In the Choose Profile dialog box, in the Profile Name drop-down list, select Outlook and then click OK.

4. In Outlook, from the Tools menu, select Options.

5. In the Options dialog box, in the Other tab, select the Empty The Deleted Items Folder Upon Exiting check box, as seen below.

Setting Automatic Archiving Options

The following procedure will move older e-mails to a separate file for archiving.

1. In the Other tab, click AutoArchive.

2. In the AutoArchive dialog box, clear the Prompt Before AutoArchive Runs check box. In the Default Folder Settings For Archiving section, in the Clean Out Items Older Than selection box, select 1 Months.

3. Click Apply These Settings To All Folders Now, as shown below, and then click OK.

Compacting Outlook Data

The following steps will reduce the size of the current e-mail store.

1. In the Options dialog box, in the Mail Setup tab, click Data Files.

2. In the Outlook Data Files dialog box, click Settings.

3. In the Personal Folders dialog box, click Compact Now, as shown below.
   Compacting time will vary with the size of the .pst file.

NOTE   *Sometimes compacting .pst files can repair faults in the files.*

4. In the Personal Folders dialog box, click OK.

5. In the Outlook Data Files dialog box, click Close.

6. In the Options dialog box, click Cancel.

LAB REVIEW QUESTIONS

Estimated completion time: 15 minutes

1. How can e-mail accounts be kept separate when accessed from the same
   user account on the same machine?

2. What method for backing up Outlook data was used in this lab?

3. What difference in the Inboxes is immediately apparent when using an
   IMAP versus a POP3 mail client?

4. How many .pst files does an Outlook IMAP e-mail client create by
   default?

5. A client has a 4-GB .pst file, and has never performed any maintenance
   on Outlook. What could you recommend to reduce the size of the .pst
   file?

6. What is the type of server that was configured in this lab as the News
   server?

LAB CHALLENGE: CONFIGURING OUTLOOK EXPRESS AS AN E-MAIL CLIENT

Estimated completion time: 25 minutes

NOTE   For this lab challenge, be sure to use your Test account.

A newly created division of Consolidated Messenger requires e-mail access. For budget reasons, this new department will be using Microsoft Outlook Express as its e-mail client. Furthermore, the users will be asked to configure Outlook Express themselves, according to your instructions. You need to create detailed instructions in WordPad on how to configure Outlook Express as a POP3, IMAP, and Simple Mail Transfer Protocol (SMTP) client. You also need to include instructions on testing the account and backing up e-mail messages.

When you are finished, e-mail your answer as an attachment from Outlook Express to Instructor@contoso.com, with the subject line Lab 4 from Student*xx*, where Student*xx* is your student account user name.

LAB 5
CONFIGURING INTERNET EXPLORER

This lab contains the following exercises and activities, some of which are optional:

- Exercise 5.1: Setting a Home Page
- Exercise 5.2: Configuring Accessibility
- Exercise 5.3: Adding Languages (Optional)
- Exercise 5.4: Viewing History (Optional)
- Exercise 5.5: Common Settings
- Exercise 5.6: Managing Favorites
- Exercise 5.7: Using Group Policy Settings for Internet Explorer
- Exercise 5.8: Maintaining Internet Explorer
- Exercise 5.9: Securing Internet Explorer
- Exercise 5.10: Submitting Your Work
- Lab Review Questions
- Lab Challenge 5.1: Configuring Internet Explorer to Work with Other Programs
- Lab Challenge 5.2: Customizing Security Zones

BEFORE YOU BEGIN

If you have not installed and configured Microsoft Office Outlook 2003 according to Lab 4, Exercises 4.1 and 4.2, you must complete those exercises before you can complete this lab.

SCENARIO

You are a Tier 1 technical support agent at Consolidated Messenger, a courier company serving metropolitan areas across the United States. The company has expanded its Internet access to more employees and there are many configuration issues that you will need to handle.

After completing this lab, you will be able to:

- Make Microsoft Internet Explorer more accessible to visually impaired users

- Configure the interface in Internet Explorer

- Manage Favorites

- Use group policy to affect the behavior of Internet Explorer for groups

- Maintain Internet Explorer

- Configure security in Internet Explorer

- Perform many other common tasks in Internet Explorer

Estimated lesson time: 115 minutes

Estimated lesson time for optional exercises: 10 minutes

EXERCISE 5.1: SETTING A HOME PAGE

Estimated completion time: 5 minutes

You would like Internet Explorer on your workstation at Consolidated Messenger to open to a Web page other than the default.

1. Log on with your student account.

2. From the Start menu, select Internet Explorer.

3. On the standard toolbar, click the Stop button (a red X).

4. In Internet Explorer, from the Tools menu, select Internet Options.

5. In the Internet Options dialog box, in the General tab, in the Home Page section, in the Address text box, type **http://support.microsoft.com**, as shown below, and click OK.

6. Click the Home icon on the standard toolbar to confirm the new home page has been set.

7. Close Internet Explorer.

EXERCISE 5.2: CONFIGURING ACCESSIBILITY

Estimated completion time: 20 minutes

An employee with poor vision needs Internet Explorer to enlarge the text when he is browsing Web pages. He has configured it to do so, but it only works on some Web pages. He also can read some fonts better than others, and would like to specify a particular font. Finally, he would like the toolbar buttons to be large, and to change the color of hyperlinks to a color he finds more visible.

Enlarging Text Size

The following steps will force Internet Explorer to use a larger font despite code to the contrary in a Web page.

1. Log on with your test account.

2. From the Start menu, select Internet Explorer.

3. In Internet Explorer, in the Address text box, type **http://www.microsoft. com** and press ENTER.

4. From the View menu, select Text Size and then select Largest.

   QUESTION   Why do the Microsoft logo and some of the text remain the same size?

5. In Internet Explorer, from the Tools menu, select Internet Options.

6. In the Internet Options dialog box, click Accessibility.

7. In the Accessibility dialog box, in the Formatting section, select the Ignore Font Sizes Specified On Web Pages check box, as shown below, and click OK. Click OK to close the Internet Options dialog box.

Changing Fonts

The following steps will force Internet Explorer to change the font of the text in a Web page regardless of code in the Web page.

1. In Internet Explorer, from the Tools menu, select Internet Options.

2. In the Internet Options dialog box, in the General tab, click Fonts.

3. In the Fonts dialog box, in the Web Page Font list, select Arial Black and click OK.

4. In the Internet Options dialog box, click OK.

   QUESTION   Why aren't the changes reflected in the Web page?

5. From the Tools menu, select Internet Options.

6. In the Internet Options dialog box, in the General tab, click Accessibility.

7. In the Accessibility dialog box, in the Formatting section, select the Ignore Font Styles Specified On Web Pages check box, as shown below, and click OK. Observe the change in the font in your browser.

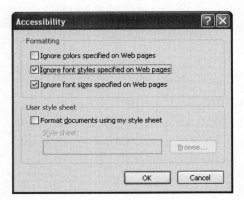

Changing Colors

The following steps will change the color in which hyperlinks appear.

1. In the Internet Options dialog box, in the General tab, click Colors.

2. In the Colors dialog box, click the Unvisited color swatch.

3. In the Color selector box, in the Basic Colors section, select the hot pink color swatch. Click OK.

4. In the Colors dialog box, click OK.

5. In the Internet Options dialog box, in the General tab, click Accessibility.

6. In the Accessibility dialog box, in the Formatting section, select the Ignore Colors Specified On Web Pages check box. Click OK.

7. In the Internet Options dialog box, click OK. Observe the new color of the hyperlinks.

8. Take a snapshot of the Internet Explorer window and paste it into a WordPad document called Student*xx*-Lab 5 in Shared Documents, where Student*xx* is your student account user name.

Changing Toolbar Icon Sizes

The following steps will change the size of the icons displayed in the toolbars in Internet Explorer.

1. Right-click the standard toolbar and select Customize.

2. In the Customize Toolbar dialog box, in the Icon Options drop-down list, select Small Icons. Click Close.

3. Change the Toolbar Icon size back to large.

4. In the Internet Options dialog box, click Close.

   NOTE Before continuing with the exercises in this lab, you might want to reset the accessibility options and the font size option back to the original values, so that Web pages are displayed correctly.

   NOTE Because this lab is long, the following exercise is optional. It can be skipped without consequence to other exercises in this lab or future labs.

EXERCISE 5.3: ADDING LANGUAGES (OPTIONAL)

Estimated completion time: 5 minutes

A multilingual employee would like to be shown how to add languages in Internet Explorer. The following steps demonstrate this task.

1. Log on with your test account.

2. From the Start menu, select Internet Explorer.

3. In Internet Explorer, from the Tools menu, select Internet Options.

4. In the Internet Options dialog box, click Languages.

5. In the Languages Preference dialog box, click Add.

6. In the Add Language dialog box, select a language, as shown below, and click OK.

7. In the Languages Preference dialog box, click Cancel (if you wanted to add the language preference, you would click OK).

8. In the Internet Options dialog box, click OK.

9. Close Internet Explorer.

> **NOTE** Because this lab is long, the following exercise is optional. It can be skipped without consequence to other exercises in this lab or future labs.

EXERCISE 5.4: VIEWING HISTORY (OPTIONAL)

Estimated completion time: 5 minutes

A user at Consolidated Messenger visited a site on the Microsoft Support Web site first thing this morning and is unable to locate it again. You need to configure her system so that the site is listed at the top of her History list.

Another employee is using his laptop for a presentation in which he is going to use the History toolbar. He wants the history list to be cleared so that only Web sites he visits during the presentation will be listed. Furthermore, he wants only sites from the last five days he has visited to be tracked.

Changing History Order

The following steps will change the order in which history is viewed in Internet Explorer.

1. Log on with your test account.

2. From the Start menu, select Internet Explorer.

3. In Internet Explorer, to create a browsing history, browse to about 10 separate pages within the support.microsoft.com Web space.

4. On the standard toolbar, click the History button (a clock with an arrow curving counterclockwise).

5. On the History toolbar, in the View drop-down list, select By Order Visited Today.

Deleting and Configuring the History List

The following steps will alter the duration that Internet Explorer uses to track
browsing history.

1. In Internet Explorer, from the Tools menu, select Internet Options.

2. In the Internet Options dialog box, in the History section, click Clear
History.

3. In the Internet Options message box, click Yes.

4. In the Internet Options dialog box, in the Days To Keep Pages In History
box, select 5, as shown below. Click OK.

EXERCISE 5.5: COMMON SETTINGS

Estimated completion time: 15 minutes
To make key employees at Consolidated Messenger familiar with Internet Explorer,
you have been asked to give a presentation outlining some common settings.

Related Information Button

The following steps will add the Related Information button to the standard toolbar.

1. Log on with your test account.

2. From the Start menu, select Internet Explorer.

3. In Internet Explorer, right-click the standard toolbar, and select Customize.

4. In the Customize Toolbar dialog box, in the Available Toolbar Buttons list, select the Related button and click Add, as shown below. Click Close.

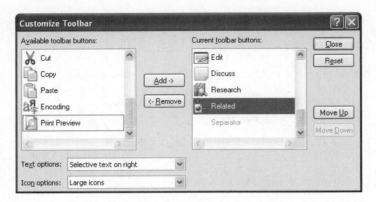

5. Ensure that the Address text box reads *http://support.microsoft.com*. Click the Related icon on the standard toolbar.

6. Take a snapshot of the Internet Explorer window, and paste it into the Student*xx*-Lab 5 WordPad document created earlier.

Accessing Folders from Internet Explorer

The following steps will allow you to browse through folders using Internet Explorer.

1. In Internet Explorer, right-click the standard toolbar and select Customize.

2. In the Customize Toolbar dialog box, in the Available Toolbar Buttons list, select the Folders button and click Add. Click Close.

3. In Internet Explorer, on the standard toolbar, click Folders.

4. Navigate to C:\Documents and Settings\Test\Favorites.

5. Take a snapshot of the Internet Explorer window and paste it into the Student*xx*-Lab 5 WordPad document created earlier.

6. Close Internet Explorer.

Starting Internet Explorer with a Blank Home Page

The following procedure will allow you to start Internet Explorer without loading the home page, and to configure Internet Explorer to always start with a blank page.

1. From the Start menu, select Run. In the Run dialog box, in the Open text box, type **iexplore -nohome** and press ENTER.

2. In Internet Explorer, from the Tools menu, select Internet Options.

QUESTION   What happens when you select Internet Options from the Tools menu?

3. In Internet Explorer, on the standard toolbar, click the Home button and then click the Stop button.

4. From the Tools menu, select Internet Options.

5. In the Internet Options dialog box, in the General tab, in the Home Page section, click Use Blank, as shown below. Click OK.

Configuring the Search Toolbar

The following steps will configure the Search button on the standard toolbar in Internet Explorer.

1. On the standard toolbar, click the Search button.

2. On the Search Companion toolbar, click Change Preferences.

3. On the How Do You Want To Use Search Companion page, click Change Internet Search Behavior.

4. On the Internet Search Behavior page, in the Select A Default Search Engine list box, select Google. Click OK.

5. Close the Search Companion toolbar.

6. On the standard toolbar, click the Search button.

7. In the What Are You Looking For text box, type **Microsoft support** and click Search.

8. Close Internet Explorer.

EXERCISE 5.6: MANAGING FAVORITES

Estimated completion time: 30 minutes

Throughout Consolidated Messenger, there are many requests dealing with the configuration of Favorites in Internet Explorer. You have had to attend to a wide variety of requests concerning this topic since the employees were granted Internet access.

Adding Items to Favorites

The following steps will add to Favorites in Internet Explorer using three different methods.

1. Log on with your student account.

2. From the Start menu, select Internet Explorer.

3. In Internet Explorer, on the Standard toolbar, click Favorites.

4. In the Address text box, type **http://support.microsoft.com**. Press ENTER.

5. Press CTRL + D to add support.microsoft.com to the Favorites toolbar.

   QUESTION   What did Microsoft Explorer name the link added to the Favorites toolbar?

   QUESTION   Where did this title come from? (Hint: From the View menu, select Source.)

6. On the Favorites toolbar, right-click Microsoft Help And Support, and select Rename. Rename the link to Microsoft Support.

7. Browse to another page within support.microsoft.com.

8. From the Favorites menu, select Add To Favorites.

9. In the Add Favorite dialog box, in the Name text box, give the link a logical name different from the default. Click OK.

10. Browse to another site within support.microsoft.com.

11. In the Address text box, drag the e icon to the Favorites toolbar.

12. Close Internet Explorer.

Manually Editing Favorites

An employee who frequently references financial information stored within the company's intranet would like to be able to easily access the calculator from Internet Explorer.

The following steps create a shortcut in Favorites in Internet Explorer.

1. From the Start menu, select My Computer.

2. Browse to the folder C:\Document and Settings\Student*xx*\Favorites.

3. In the Favorites folder, from the File menu, select New and then select Shortcut.

4. In the Create Shortcut dialog box, in the Type The Location Of This Item text box, type **C:\windows\system32\calc.exe**, as shown below, and click Next.

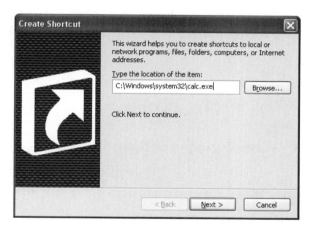

5. On the Select A Title For The Program page, in the Type A Name For This Shortcut text box, type **Calculator** and click Finish.

6. Close the Favorites folder.

7. From the Start menu, select Internet Explorer.

8. In Internet Explorer, on the Favorites toolbar, click Calculator.

9. Close Calculator.

Configuring a Favorite for Offline Use

An executive at Consolidated Messenger often leaves the office in the afternoon and brings his laptop home. He doesn't have Internet access at home and wants to be able to browse a particular site in his Favorites while offline. Furthermore, when this site changes, he wants to be notified by e-mail.

The following procedure will configure Internet Explorer to cache a Web page according to a specified schedule. It will also configure Internet Explorer to notify you by e-mail when a particular Web page changes.

1. In Internet Explorer, on the Favorites toolbar, click Organize.

2. In the Organize Favorites dialog box, select Microsoft Support. In the Microsoft Support section, select the Make Available Offline check box, as shown below, and click Properties.

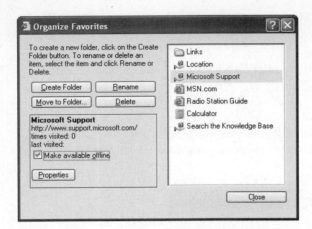

3. In the Microsoft Support Properties dialog box, in the Schedule tab, under Synchronize This Favorite, select Using The Following Schedule. Click Add.

4. In the New Schedule dialog box, in the Every text box, enter **1**. In the Time text box, enter **8:15 AM**.

5. In the Name text box, type **Microsoft Support Update Schedule**, as shown below. Click OK.

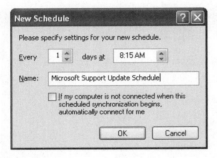

6. In the Microsoft Support Properties dialog box, in the Download tab, select the When This Page Changes, Send E-Mail To check box. In the E-Mail Address text box, type **Student*xx*@contoso.com**. In the Mail Server (SMTP) text box, type **Server**. Click OK.

7. In the Organize Favorites dialog box, click Close.

8. Close Internet Explorer.

Importing Favorites

An employee at Consolidated Messenger has been given a new computer. She needs to have access to the Favorites she had on her old computer. Another technical support employee copied her old Favorites to a network share.

In the following steps, you will transfer Favorites from one instance of Internet Explorer to another.

> **NOTE**   For this exercise, you will need a partner.

1. Log on with your administrator account (the password is P@ssw0rd).

2. From the Start menu, select My Computer. Browse to the folder C:\ Documents and Settings\Student*xx*, where Student*xx* is your student account user name.

3. Right-click Favorites and select Copy.

4. In the Other Places section on the left, click Shared Documents.

5. In the Shared Documents folder, from the File menu, select New and then select Folder. Name the new folder Old Favorites.

6. Right-click Old Favorites and select Properties.

7. In the Old Favorites Properties dialog box, in the Sharing tab, in the Network Sharing And Security section, select the Share This Folder On The Network check box. Click OK.

8. In the Sharing message box, click Yes.

9. Open the Old Favorites folder. In the Old Favorites folder, from the Edit menu, select Paste.

10. In the Old Favorites folder, in the Other Places section on the left, click My Network Places.

11. In the My Network Places folder, open Old Favorites On Computer*xx*, where Computer*xx* is your partner's computer.

12. In the Old Favorites On Computer*xx* folder, select Favorites and press CTRL + C.

13. In the Other Places section on the left, click My Computer.

14. Browse to the folder C:\Documents and Settings\Student*xx*, where Student*xx* is your student account user name. Press CTRL + V.

15. In the Confirm Folder Replace message box, click Yes To All.

16. Log off and log on with your student account.

17. From the Start menu, select Internet Explorer. Your Favorites should now be the Favorites that your partner's student account contained.

EXERCISE 5.7: USING GROUP POLICY SETTINGS FOR INTERNET EXPLORER

Estimated completion time: 5 minutes

Management has decided that all users are to initially have the same home page. Also, the title bar of Internet Explorer is to be customized to include the company name.

The following steps will implement these changes via group policy.

1. Log on with your administrator account (the password is P@ssw0rd).

2. From the Start menu, select Run. In the Run dialog box, in the Open text box, type **gpedit.msc** and press ENTER.

3. In the Group Policy console, under the User Configuration node, expand Windows Settings. Expand Internet Explorer Maintenance, and select URLs, as shown below.

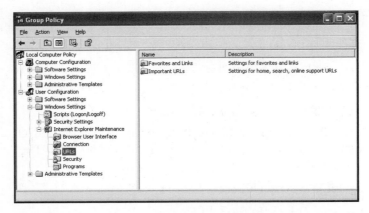

4. In the details pane, in the Name column, double-click Important URLs.

5. In the Important URLs dialog box, select the Customize Home Page URL check box. In the Home Page URL text box, type **http://www.consolidated messenger.com**. Click OK.

6. In the Group Policy console, under the Internet Explorer Maintenance node, select Browser User Interface.

7. In the details pane, in the Name column, double-click Browser Title.

8. In the Browser Title dialog box, select the Customize Title Bars check box. In the Title Bar Text text box, type **Consolidated Messenger**. Click OK.

9. Log off and log back on with your student account.

10. From the Start menu, select Internet Explorer. Take a snapshot of Internet Explorer and paste it into the Student*xx*-Lab 5 WordPad document created earlier.

EXERCISE 5.8: MAINTAINING INTERNET EXPLORER

Estimated completion time: 10 minutes
Technical support management at Consolidated Messenger has asked you to implement and demonstrate Internet Explorer maintenance tasks to the employees with Internet access.

Deleting Temporary Internet Files Manually

The following steps will delete temporary files used by Internet Explorer.

1. Log on with your administrator account (the password is P@ssw0rd).

2. From the Start menu, select Internet Explorer.

3. In Internet Explorer, from the Tools menu, select Internet Options.

4. In the Internet Options dialog box, in the General tab, in the Temporary Internet Files section, click Settings.

5. In the Settings dialog box, click View Files.

6. In the Temporary Internet Files folder, from the Edit menu, select Select All. Press the DELETE key.

7. In the Warning message box, click Yes. Close the Temporary Internet Files folder. In the Settings dialog box, click OK.

Automatically Deleting Temporary Internet Files on Exiting Internet Explorer

A user who visits proprietary Web sites wants to make sure that no temporary files from those sites remain on his computer when he exits Internet Explorer.

The following steps will ensure that temporary Internet files are deleted on exiting Internet Explorer.

1. In the Internet Options dialog box, select the Advanced tab.

2. In the Settings list, in the Security section, select the Empty Temporary Internet Files Folder When Browser Is Closed check box, as shown below.

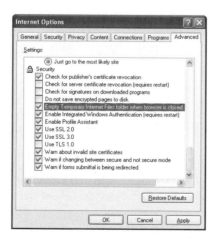

Deleting Cookies

You have received a warning from technical support management that a site popular among the bicycle messengers might contain malicious cookies.

The following steps will delete the cookies stored on your computer.

1. In the Internet Options dialog box, in the General tab, in the Temporary Internet Files section, click Delete Cookies.

2. In the Delete Cookies message box, click OK.

Changing the Cached Pages Update Settings

The following steps will alter how often the cache for a Web site will be updated.

1. In the Internet Options dialog box, in the General tab, in the Temporary Internet Files section, click Settings.

2. In the Settings dialog box, under Check For Newer Versions Of Stored Pages, select Every Visit To The Page, as shown below. Click OK. In the Internet Options dialog box, click OK.

3. Close Internet Explorer.

EXERCISE 5.9: SECURING INTERNET EXPLORER

Estimated completion time: 10 minutes

Technical support management has given you the task of ensuring the security surrounding Internet access. To implement security, you will need to adjust the security zones and cookie acceptance.

Configuring Security Zones

The following steps will adjust the security level for a particular security zone, create a trusted site within this zone, and allow you to observe the effects.

1. Log on with your test account.

2. From the Start menu, select Internet Explorer.

3. In the Internet Options dialog box, in the Security tab, in the Security Level For This Zone section, click Default Level.

4. Move the slider to the High position. Click Apply. Click Custom Level.

   QUESTION Does the High security level allow downloads?

5. In the Security Settings dialog box, click Cancel.

6. In the Internet Options dialog box, in the Select A Web Content Zone To Specify Its Security Settings section, select Trusted Sites.

7. In the Security Level For This Zone section, click Default Level.

8. In the Trusted Sites section, click Sites.

9. In the Trusted Sites dialog box, in the Add This Web Site To The Zone text box, type **https://www.microsoft.com**. Click Add, as shown below. Click OK. Click OK to close the Internet Options dialog box.

10. In Internet Explorer, in the Address text box, type **http://www.google.com** and press ENTER.

11. On the Google Web page, right-click any hyperlink and select Save Target As. In the Security Alert message box, click OK.

12. In the Address text box, type **https://www.microsoft.com** and press ENTER.

13. On the Microsoft Web page, right-click any hyperlink and select Save Target As. In the Save As dialog box, click Cancel.

Setting Cookie Options to Secure Privacy

To prevent cookies from reporting information to a third party, you need to adjust the cookie options in Internet Explorer.

The following steps will create a low tolerance for cookie adoption.

1. In Internet Explorer, from the Tools menu, select Internet Options.

2. In the Internet Options dialog box, in the Privacy tab, in the Settings section, move the slider to High. Click OK.

   QUESTION What two sets of cookies does this setting block?

EXERCISE 5.10: SUBMITTING YOUR WORK

Estimated completion time: 5 minutes
The following exercise allows you to submit the work you completed in this lab to your instructor.

1. Log on with your student account.

2. E-mail the Student*xx*-Lab 5 WordPad document as an attachment to Instructor@contoso.com with the subject line Student*xx*-Lab 5 *Your Name*, where Student*xx* is your student account user name.

LAB REVIEW QUESTIONS

Estimated completion time: 15 minutes
1. A user finds a Web site that was previously available offline unavailable. Recently, a friend "freed up some space." What folder was emptied to cause this problem?

2. What setting in Internet Explorer, in your test account, would allow the hyperlink to be saved in Exercise 5.10?

3. What can be used to define the behavior of Internet Explorer for particular groups or users?

4. How and where does Internet Explorer store Favorites?

5. How can Internet Explorer be configured to easily browse folders?

6. In Exercise 5.9, why were you able to copy a hyperlink from *www.microsoft.com* but not from *www.google.com*, when they were in the same security zone?

LAB CHALLENGE 5.1: CONFIGURING INTERNET EXPLORER TO WORK WITH OTHER PROGRAMS

Estimated completion time: 5 minutes

An employee who maintains the company Web site would like Internet Explorer to be configured to work with the following programs by default:

- HTML editor: Notepad
- E-mail client: Hotmail
- Newsgroup reader: Outlook Express
- Internet call: NetMeeting
- Calendar: Microsoft Office Outlook
- Contact list: Address Book

Use your student account to complete the lab challenge.

LAB CHALLENGE 5.2: CUSTOMIZING SECURITY ZONES

Estimated completion time: 15 minutes

In order to ensure security in Internet Explorer, you need to customize the Internet, Local Intranet, and Trusted Sites security zones. Use your test account for this lab challenge.

For the Internet zone, configure the following:

- Do not allow components not signed with Authenticode to run without the user expressly indicating it is okay in response to a prompt.
- Disable all ActiveX controls and plug-ins.
- Disallow downloads.
- Set Software Channel permissions to the highest safety level.

For the Local Intranet zone, configure the following:

- Enable all ActiveX controls and plug-ins.
- Force the user to log on with a user name and password.

Add Microsoft's homepage, TechNet, and *support.microsoft.com* to the Trusted Sites Zone. Disable all ActiveX controls and plug-ins for the Trusted Sites.

INSTALLING AND CONFIGURING THE MICROSOFT OFFICE SYSTEM

This lab contains the following exercises and activities:

- Exercise 6.1: Checking System Requirements Using MSinfo32
- Exercise 6.2: Creating and Using a System Restore Point
- Exercise 6.3: Installing Microsoft Office Professional Edition 2003
- Exercise 6.4: Configuring Program Compatibility
- Exercise 6.5: Adding and Using a Toolbar
- Exercise 6.6: Creating a Custom Toolbar
- Exercise 6.7: Configuring Microsoft Word
- Exercise 6.8: Adding Items to a Menu List
- Exercise 6.9: Submitting Your Work
- Lab Review Questions
- Lab Challenge: Configuring a Group Project for Microsoft Office Excel 2003

BEFORE YOU BEGIN

If you have not completed "Exercise 3.3: Configuring Quick Launch," or the "Before You Begin" exercises in Lab 4, you will need to complete the following steps, which will create a shared folder.

1. Log on with your administrator account.

2. From the Start menu, select My Computer, and open Shared Documents.

3. In the Shared Documents folder, from the File menu, select New, and then select Folder. For the folder name, type **Share** and press ENTER.

4. Right-click the Share folder and select Properties.

5. In the Share Properties, in the Sharing tab, in the Network Sharing And Security section, select the Share This Folder On The Network check

box. Also select the Allow Network Users To Change My Files check box. Click OK.

NOTE   Before completing step 5, you might need to click If You Understand The Security Risks But Want To Share Files Without Running The Wizard, Click Here, and in the subsequent Enable File Sharing message box, select Just Enable File Sharing and click OK.

If you have not installed and configured Microsoft Office Outlook 2003 according to Lab 4, Exercises 4.1 and 4.2, or according to the "Before You Begin" section of Lab 5, you must complete those exercises before you can complete this lab.

SCENARIO

You are a Tier 1 technical support agent serving internal clients at Contoso, an insurance company. Contoso has upgraded many of its systems, and Microsoft Office Professional Edition 2003 needs to be installed and configured.

After completing this lab, you will be able to:

- Check system requirements
- Create and restore to a system restore point
- Perform a custom install of Microsoft Office Professional Edition 2003
- Configure program compatibility settings
- Customize and configure Microsoft Office products

Estimated lesson time: 95 minutes

EXERCISE 6.1: CHECKING SYSTEM REQUIREMENTS USING MSINFO32

Estimated completion time: 10 minutes

You are a Tier 1 technical support agent for Contoso, an insurance company. Many of the computer systems have been upgraded to Microsoft Windows XP, and await installation of Office 2003. You have been asked to probe a system to see if it meets recommended system requirements for Office 2003.

1. Log on with your student account.

2. From the Start menu, select Run. In the Run dialog box, in the Open text box, type **msinfo32**, and press ENTER.

3. In the System Information dialog box, explore the console tree and note the following information in a WordPad document saved in Shared Documents with the name Student*xx*-Lab 6. An example of System Information on a hard drive is given after the bulleted list.

   ❑ Operating system

   ❑ Processor

- ❑ Total physical memory
- ❑ Free space on your hard drive

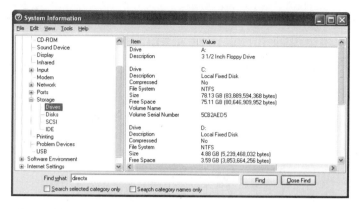

4. Close all open windows. From the Start menu, select Internet Explorer.

5. In Internet Explorer, ensure that *http://www.microsoft.com* is in the Address text box.

6. In the Search Microsoft.com For text box (upper-right corner of the Web page), type **Office 2003 system requirements** and press ENTER.

7. In the Product Information section, click the link entitled Office 2003 Editions System Requirements. If the search did not find this link, go to *http://www.microsoft.com/office/editions/prodinfo/sysreq.mspx*

8. Under Office 2003 Editions System Requirements, click Office Professional Edition 2003 System Requirements.

QUESTION   Does your computer meet the system requirements of Microsoft Office 2003?

9. Close Internet Explorer.

EXERCISE 6.2: CREATING AND USING A SYSTEM RESTORE POINT

Estimated completion time: 10 minutes

You have set up a test system with identical hardware to many of the computers at Contoso. You have been assigned the task of installing Office 2003 on the computer and recording any problems. These results will be used to avoid the same problems during the company-wide installation.

Before you begin the installation, you want to create a system restore point. This way, if there is a disaster during installation, you can return to a clean system configuration.

1. Log on with your administrator account (the password is P@ssw0rd).

2. From the Start menu, select Help And Support.

3. In the Help And Support Center, in the Pick A Help Topic section, click Performance And Maintenance.

4. On the Performance And Maintenance page, in the Performance And Maintenance list box, select Using System Restore To Undo Changes.

5. On the Using System Restore To Undo Changes page, under Pick A Task, select Run The System Restore Wizard.

6. In the System Restore Wizard, on the Welcome To System Restore page, under To Begin, Select The Task That You Want To Perform, select Create A Restore Point. Click Next.

7. On the Create A Restore Point page, in the Restore Point Description text box, type **Before Microsoft Office 2003 Install**, as shown below. Click Create.

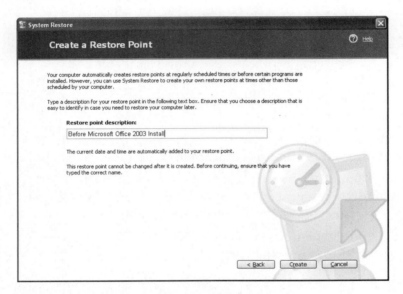

8. On the Restore Point Created page, click Close.

NOTE *The following steps are not made for a practical purpose; we are going to restore the system to the point we just created without committing any intervening actions. The purpose of the next steps is to familiarize you with the task of using the System Restore Wizard to restore the operating system to a particular point.*

9. In the Help And Support Center, on the Using System Restore To Undo Changes page, under Pick A Task, select Run The System Restore Wizard.

10. In the System Restore Wizard, on the Welcome To System Restore page, under To Begin, Select The Task That You Want To Perform, verify that Restore My Computer To An Earlier Time is selected. Click Next.

11. On the Select A Restore Point page, verify that the restore point you just created is selected in the On This List, Click A Restore Point list, as shown below. Click Next.

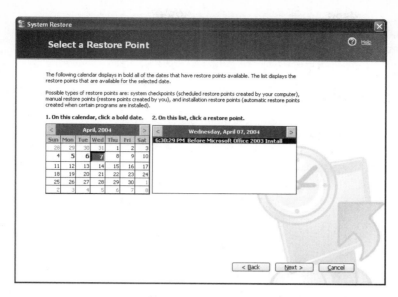

12. On the Confirm Restore Point Selection page, click Next.

13. Windows will restart. Log on with your administrator account.

14. The System Restore Wizard will open. On the Restoration Complete page, click OK.

EXERCISE 6.3: INSTALLING MICROSOFT OFFICE PROFESSIONAL EDITION 2003

Estimated completion time: 10 minutes

Having successfully created and tested a system restore point, you are now ready to install Office 2003.

1. Log on with your administrator account (the password is P@ssw0rd).

2. Insert your Microsoft Office Professional Edition 2003 CD into the CD-ROM drive.

3. In the Office11 (D:) window, double-click Setup.

4. In the Microsoft Office 2003 Setup wizard, on the Maintenance Mode Options page, select Add Or Remove Features and click Next.

5. On the Custom Setup page, select the check boxes for all of the applications, and also select the Choose Advanced Customization Of Applications check box, as shown below. Click Next.

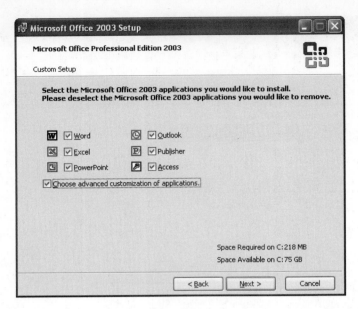

6. On the Advanced Customization page, in the Choose Installation Options For Applications And Tools section, in the Microsoft Office drop-down list, select Run All From My Computer, as shown below. Click Update.

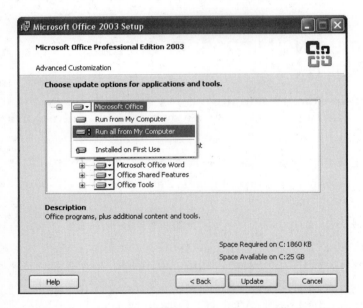

7. On the Now Updating Office page, the Installation Progress is displayed. Installation will take three minutes or more. When installation is complete, the Microsoft Office 2003 Setup message box appears, stating that the update completed successfully. Click OK to close the message box.

EXERCISE 6.4: CONFIGURING PROGRAM COMPATIBILITY

Estimated completion time: 5 minutes

There would never be a circumstance using Office 2003 under Windows XP in which you would need to alter the operating system compatibility settings, because they are fully compatible. You are altering the settings here simply as practice with the interface.

Most programs will not require configuration of these settings. Exceptions will be primarily legacy programs designed for specific industries, and older games.

1. Log on with your test account.

2. From the Start menu, select My Computer.

3. Browse to the folder C:\Program Files\Microsoft Office\Office11.

4. Locate and right-click the file named WINWORD, and select Properties.

5. In the WINWORD Properties dialog box, in the Compatibility tab, in the Compatibility Mode section, select the Run This Program In Compatibility Mode For check box, and in the drop-down list, select Windows 95, as shown below. Click OK.

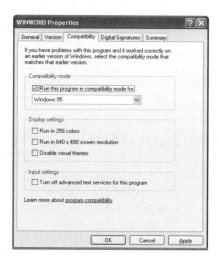

EXERCISE 6.5: ADDING AND USING A TOOLBAR

Estimated completion time: 10 minutes
An employee at Contoso who specializes in proofreading documents written by other employees would like the reviewing commands of Microsoft Word to be more accessible.

NOTE   The following steps require a partner.

1. Log on with your student account.

2. From the Start menu, select All Programs, Microsoft Office, and select Microsoft Office Word 2003.

QUESTION   Which toolbars are displayed by default?

3. In Microsoft Word, type **Here is some text ready for you're review**.

4. From the File menu, select Save As. In the Save As dialog box, browse to the Share folder in Shared Documents. In the File Name text box, type **sample document** and click Save.

   NOTE Wait until your partner has completed steps 1 through 4.

5. From the File menu, select Close.

6. From the File menu, select Open.

7. In the Open dialog box, in the File Name text box, type **computer.xx**\ **share****sample document**, where **computer.xx** is the name of your partner's computer. Click Open.

8. Right-click the standard toolbar, and select Reviewing.

9. On the Reviewing toolbar, click the Track Changes button (hint: hovering the mouse over a button summons a ScreenTip that identifies the name of each button).

10. In the document, replace *you're* with *your*. Highlight *your*, and on the Reviewing toolbar, click the Insert Comment button.

11. In the Comment text box, type "**your" is the possessive, not "you're"**.

12. From the File menu, select Save. Close Microsoft Word.

EXERCISE 6.6: CREATING A CUSTOM TOOLBAR

Estimated completion time: 10 minutes
An employee at Contoso uses certain commands in Word many times a day, and would like them to be brought together into one custom toolbar.

1. Log on with your student account.

2. From the Start menu, select All Programs, Microsoft Office, and then select Microsoft Office Word 2003.

3. In Word 2003, right-click any toolbar and select Customize.

4. In the Customize dialog box, in the Toolbars tab, click New.

5. In the New Toolbar dialog box, in the Toolbar Name text box, type **Classroom**, as shown below. Click OK.

6. In the Customize dialog box, in the Commands tab, in the Categories list, select File. In the Commands list, drag Check Out and Check In to the newly created Classroom toolbar.

7. In the Categories list, select Window And Help. In the Commands window, drag Microsoft Office Word Help to the Classroom toolbar. After adding all commands, your Classroom toolbar should look like the one below.

8. In the Customize dialog box, click Close.

9. Drag the Classroom toolbar to the toolbar area at the top of the Microsoft Word window, and dock it there.

EXERCISE 6.7: CONFIGURING MICROSOFT WORD

Estimated completion Time: 20 minutes

You have been asked by the Human Resources department to give a presentation on the Microsoft Office System in the hopes that it will increase productivity.

Creating a New Document from a Template

Office offers a wide array of templates for many types of documents, the use of which can save a lot of time.

1. Log on with your student account.

2. From the Start menu, select All Programs, Microsoft Office, and then select Microsoft Office Word 2003.

3. In the Getting Started task pane, in the drop-down list at the top, select New Document.

4. In the New Document task pane, under Templates, click On My Computer.

5. In the Templates dialog box, in the Publications tab, select Brochure. Under Create New, ensure that Document is selected, as shown below. Click OK.

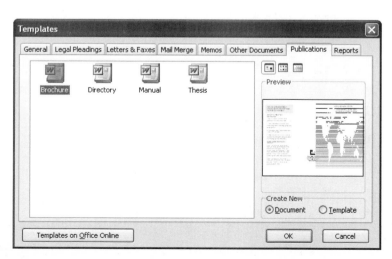

Viewing Formatting Marks

When you are trying to get a document to look the way you want, it is sometimes useful to view the formatting marks, which reveal in part how Word is being told to arrange a document.

1. From the Tools menu, select Options.

2. In the Options dialog box, in the View tab, under Formatting Marks, select All. Click OK. Observe the effect on the brochure opened in the previous task.

Altering Selection Behavior

When dealing with some documents, particularly technical documents, you often want to select only part of a word.

1. In the Options dialog box, select the Edit tab.

2. Under Editing Options, clear the When Selecting, Automatically Select Entire Word check box.

Changing Printing Settings

On some noncolor printers, trying to print colors as shades of gray leads to poor print quality. This can be mitigated by printing colors as black. This is mostly a problem on older, lower resolution printers.

1. In the Options dialog box, select the Compatibility tab.

2. In the Options list, select Print Colors As Black On Noncolor Printers check box, as shown below.

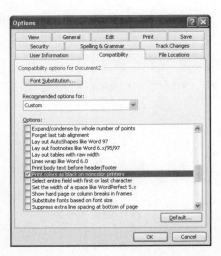

Changing File Locations to a Network Share

To more easily collaborate with others on documents, it is often useful to store certain files on a network share.

1. In the File Locations tab, under File Locations, in the File Types Column, select Documents. Click Modify.

2. In the Modify Location dialog box, in the Folder Name text box, type **\\Computer*xx*\share**, where **Computer*xx*** is the name of your partner's computer. Click OK.

Altering Markup Settings

It might be easier to view markups by using different styles to display them.

1. In the Options dialog box, select the Track Changes tab.

2. In the Track Changes tab, under Markup, in the Deletions drop-down list, select Double Underline, as seen below.

Configuring Proofing Tools

The following steps configure three separate proofing tools.

Many people dislike it when Word changes words as they are typed; this feature can be disabled.

There are many words organizations use that are not in a dictionary. To prevent Word from marking these words as misspelled, you can add them to the custom dictionary.

It is possible to modify what the grammar and style checker checks.

1. In the Spelling And Grammar tab, under Spelling, clear the Check Spelling As You Type check box. Under Grammar, clear the Check Grammar As You Type check box.

2. Under Spelling, click Custom Dictionaries.

3. In the Custom Dictionaries dialog box, in the Dictionary List, ensure that Custom.dic is selected, and click Modify.

   QUESTION   *What words have automatically been added to Custom.dic?*

4. In the Custom.dic dialog box, in the Word text box, type **Contoso** and click Add.

5. In the Custom.dic dialog box, click OK.

6. In the Custom Dictionaries dialog box, click OK.

7. In the Options dialog box, under Grammar, click Settings.

8. In the Grammar Settings dialog box, ensure that the Writing Style drop-down list has Grammar Only selected.

9. In the Grammar And Style Options list, under Style, select the Clichés, Colloquialisms, And Jargon check box. Also select the Sentence Length (More Than Sixty Words) and Use Of First Person check boxes, as shown below. Click OK.

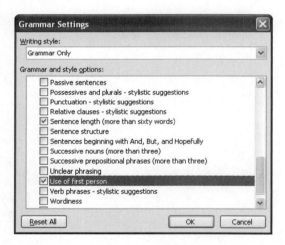

10. In the Options dialog box, click OK.

Configuring AutoCorrect Options

AutoCorrect options are useful, but sometimes they have unintended consequences. For example, not all mentions of URLs need to be turned into active hyperlinks.

1. From the Tools menu, select Auto Correct Options.

2. In the AutoCorrect dialog box, in the AutoFormat tab, under Replace, clear the Internet And Network Paths With Hyperlinks check box.

3. In the AutoCorrect tab, clear the Correct Two Initial Capitals and Replace Text As You Type check boxes. Click OK.

4. In the AutoFormat dialog box, click OK.

5. Close Word, and do not save changes.

EXERCISE 6.8: ADDING ITEMS TO A MENU LIST

Estimated completion time: 10 minutes

You have been asked to write several macros for the accounting department to simplify tasks they do repeatedly in preparing presentations for management. In preparation for doing this, you want to create a menu to facilitate access to the macro tools.

1. Log on with your student account.

2. From the Start menu, select All Programs, Microsoft Office, and then select Microsoft Office PowerPoint 2003.

3. Right-click the menu bar, and select Customize.

4. In the Customize dialog box, in the Commands tab, in the Categories list, select New Menu.

5. In the Commands list, drag New Menu to the end of the menu bar, just after Help.

6. In the Categories list, select Tools.

7. In the Commands list, drag Macros, Record New Macro, and Visual Basic Editor to the New menu. Click Close to close the Customize dialog box.

8. In the Menu bar, right-click New Menu and select Name: New Menu. Type **Macro** and press ENTER.

9. Take a screenshot of Microsoft PowerPoint with the new Macro menu and paste it in the Studentxx-Lab 6 WordPad document created earlier in this lab.

10. Close PowerPoint.

EXERCISE 6.9: SUBMITTING YOUR WORK

Estimated completion time: 5 minutes

The following exercise allows you to submit the work you completed in this lab to your instructor.

1. Log on with your student account.

2. E-mail the Studentxx-Lab 6 WordPad document as an attachment to Instructor@contoso.com with the subject line Studentxx-Lab 6 *Your Name*, where Studentxx is your student account user name.

LAB REVIEW QUESTIONS

Estimated completion time: 15 minutes

1. What tool did we use to determine if your computer met the system requirements to run Office 2003?

2. When running setup for Office 2003, why did we Update rather than Install?

3. What two types of programs are among the most likely to need to have compatibility settings altered?

4. Where can you configure Word to print hidden text?

5. Where can you configure Word to print colors as black?

6. What file locations can you change in Word?

7. What is the default name of the file containing custom dictionary entries?

LAB CHALLENGE: CONFIGURING A GROUP PROJECT FOR MICROSOFT OFFICE EXCEL 2003

Estimated completion time: 20 minutes

The accounting group at Contoso often has to collaborate on documents created in Excel and Word. The documents are financial and laden with XY scatter charts, line graphs, and flow charts. You need to create a custom toolbar or menu to assist in creating and editing these items.

Furthermore, accounting group members collaborate in groups on both Excel and Word. They need to be able to save and load documents from a network share. To keep strict track of what document is being worked on by whom and when, they check the documents in and out. You need to alter the file locations and create a menu or toolbar to assist with collaboration in both programs.

LAB 7

TROUBLESHOOTING OFFICE APPLICATIONS

This lab contains the following exercises and activities:

- Exercise 7.1: Restoring Default Menu Settings in Word 2003
- Exercise 7.2: Removing Unneeded Components from Microsoft Office
- Exercise 7.3: Changing Language Formats
- Exercise 7.4: Creating a Chart in Excel
- Exercise 7.5: Creating and Modifying an Excel Macro
- Exercise 7.6: Embedding and Linking Objects in Excel
- Exercise 7.7: Opening and Repairing an Office File
- Exercise 7.8: Using Microsoft Office Application Recovery
- Exercise 7.9: Configuring Backup and Recovery Settings
- Exercise 7.10: Submitting Your Work
- Lab Review Questions
- Lab Challenge: Linking and Embedding Objects in PowerPoint

BEFORE YOU BEGIN

If you have not installed and configured Microsoft Office Outlook 2003 according to Lab 4, Exercises 4.1 and 4.2, or according to the "Before You Begin" section of Lab 5 or Lab 6, you must complete those exercises before you can complete this lab.

SCENARIO

You are with technical support at Contoso, a small stock brokerage. It is your job to help employees with day-to-day issues with their computers and applications. The company has recently upgraded to the Microsoft Office System.

After completing this lab, you will be able to:

- Restore default settings for menus and toolbars
- Add or remove components of Office 2003

- Change language settings in Office 2003

- Create and modify macros in Office 2003

- Embed and link objects in Office 2003

- Recover documents and configure backup and recovery settings in Office 2003

Estimated lesson time: 90 minutes

EXERCISE 7.1: RESTORING DEFAULT MENU SETTINGS IN WORD 2003

Estimated completion time: 5 minutes

An employee has been assigned to a new department, but is keeping the same office and computer. The old department customized the menus in Microsoft Office Word 2003, but the new department uses the default menus. You need to reset the menus to their default settings.

1. Log on with your student account.

2. From the Start menu, select All Programs, Microsoft Office, and select Microsoft Office Word 2003.

3. In Microsoft Word, from the Tools menu, select Customize.

4. In the Customize dialog box, in the Commands tab, in the Categories list, select File, as shown below.

5. In the Commands list, drag Web Page Preview into the File menu and drop it under Close.

6. In the Customize dialog box, click Close.

7. From the Tools menu, select Customize.

8. In the Customize dialog box, in the Commands tab, click Rearrange Commands.

9. In the Rearrange Commands dialog box, under Choose A Menu Or Toolbar To Rearrange, verify that Menu Bar is selected. In the drop-down list adjacent to Menu Bar, verify that File is selected. Click Reset.

10. In the Reset Toolbar message box, click OK. Note that the Preview Web Page command has been removed from the File menu.

11. Close all open windows and programs. Do not save changes.

EXERCISE 7.2: REMOVING UNNEEDED COMPONENTS FROM MICROSOFT OFFICE

Estimated completion time: 5 minutes

An employee doesn't want unneeded components of Office installed, to save disk space and reduce clutter on the Start menu. However, if she does need to use those components in the future, she wants them available.

1. Log on with your administrator account (the password is P@ssw0rd).

2. From the Start menu, select Control Panel.

3. In Control Panel, double-click Add Or Remove Programs (switch to Classic view if necessary).

4. In the Add Or Remove Programs window, in the Currently Installed Programs scroll window, select Microsoft Office Professional Edition 2003. Click Change.

5. In the Microsoft Office 2003 Setup Wizard, on the Maintenance Mode Options page, verify that Add Or Remove Features is selected and click Next.

6. On the Custom Setup page, select the Choose Advanced Customizations Of Applications check box. Click Next.

7. On the Advanced Customization page, click the Microsoft Office Publisher node drop-down list, as shown below. Select Installed On First Use. Click Update.

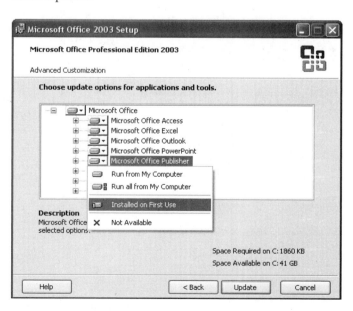

8. The Now Updating Office page measures the progress of uninstalling the component. When it is finished, a Microsoft Office 2003 Setup message box appears. Click OK.

9. Close the Add Or Remove Programs window and Control Panel.

EXERCISE 7.3: CHANGING LANGUAGE FORMATS

Estimated completion time: 5 minutes

An employee that translates Microsoft PowerPoint presentations into foreign languages needs to be able to edit multiple languages. You are not sure how this is done, so you need to use Microsoft Office Online Help to find a method.

1. Log on with your test account.

2. From the Start menu, select All Programs, Microsoft Office, and select Microsoft Office PowerPoint 2003.

3. If the task pane is not present, press CTRL + F1 to activate it.

4. In the task pane, in the drop-down list at the top, select Help.

5. In the Assistance section, in the Search For text box, type **language format**.

6. In the Results From Office Online scroll window, select Enable Editing Of Multiple Languages In Office Programs.

7. On the Enable Editing Of Multiple Languages In Office Programs help page, follow steps 1 through 4 and add the following languages.

   ❑ Croatian

   ❑ Galician

   ❑ Kyrgyz

   ❑ Tatar

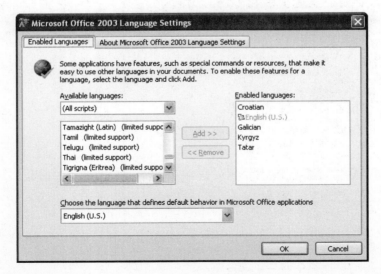

8. Take a screen shot of the Microsoft Office 2003 Language Settings dialog box, like the one above, and paste it into a WordPad document saved in

Shared Documents with the name Student*xx*-Lab 7, where Student*xx* is your student account user name.

9. Close the Microsoft Office 2003 Language Settings dialog box, dismissing the two message boxes that appear.

10. Close PowerPoint.

EXERCISE 7.4: CREATING A CHART IN EXCEL

Estimated completion time: 5 minutes

This chart is created to demonstrate macro creating, use, and editing in the subsequent exercises.

1. Log on with your student account.

2. From the Start menu, select All Programs, Microsoft Office, and select Microsoft Office Excel 2003.

3. From the File menu, select Open.

4. Navigate to Shared Documents\Lab Manual\Lab 7. Open the Lilliputian500 Microsoft Excel worksheet.

5. In Microsoft Office Excel 2003, in the Lilliputian500 worksheet, click cell A4: 31-Dec-69.

6. Scroll down to row 413, and while holding down the SHIFT key, click cell B413: 1,252.33. The block of cells from A4 to B413 should now be selected.

7. From the Insert menu, select Chart.

8. In the Chart Wizard – Step 1 Of 4 – Chart Type dialog box, in the Chart Type list, select Line. In the Chart Subtype section, select the upper left option: Line (the chart type is described below the Chart Subtype section), as shown below. Click Finish.

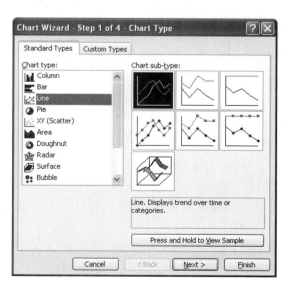

NOTE   Do not close Excel; the next exercise continues from this point.

EXERCISE 7.5: CREATING AND MODIFYING AN EXCEL MACRO

Estimated completion time: 20 minutes

A stock analyst at Contoso adds the same items to many charts each day. He would like help in creating a macro to automate this task.

> **NOTE** This exercise is a continuation of the previous exercise.

Creating a Macro in Excel

1. Select the plot line in the chart by clicking it.

2. From the Tools menu, select Macro, and select Record New Macro.

3. In the Record Macro dialog box, in the Macro Name text box, type **Trendliner**. In the Shortcut Key text box, type **t**, as shown below. Click OK.

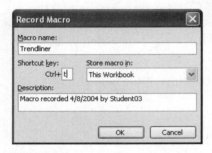

4. Right-click the plot line and select Add Trendline.

5. In the Add Trendline dialog box, in the Type tab, under Trend/Regression Type, verify that Linear is selected and click OK.

6. Right-click the plot line and select Add Trendline.

7. In the Add Trendline dialog box, in the Type tab, under Trend/Regression Type, select Moving Average. In the Period text box, type **180**. Click OK.

8. Right-click the plot line and select Add Trendline.

9. In the Add Trendline dialog box, in the Type tab, under Trend/Regression Type, select Moving Average. In the Period text box, type **130**. Click OK.

10. Right-click the plot line and select Add Trendline.

11. In the Add Trendline dialog box, in the Type tab, under Trend/Regression Type, select Moving Average. In the Period text box, type **60**. Click OK.

12. On the Stop Recording toolbar, click the Stop Recording button (the small square).

13. Click a blank area in the chart and press DELETE. This deletes the chart.

14. Re-create the chart according to steps 5 through 8 in Exercise 7-4.

Editing a Macro in Visual Basic

The following steps instruct you how to modify a macro in Visual Basic.

1. From the Tools menu, select Macro and select Macros.

2. In the Macro dialog box, verify that in the Macro Name text box Trendliner appears and click Edit.

3. In the Microsoft Visual Basic – Lilliputian500.xls window, verify that the Lilliputian500.xls – Module1 (Code) window is the active window.

4. From the Edit menu, select Find.

5. In the Find dialog box, in the Find What text box, type **130** and click Find Next.

6. Change the found instance of 130 to 120, as shown below. Click Cancel to close the Find dialog box.

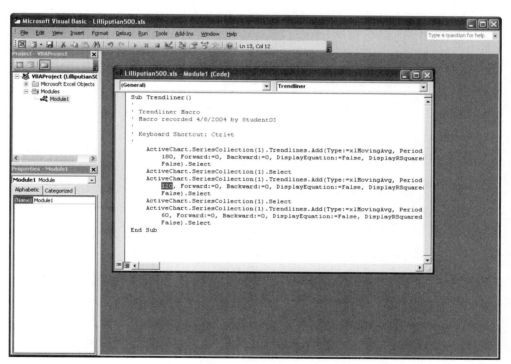

7. From the File menu, select Save Lilliputian500. Close Microsoft Visual Basic.

8. In Microsoft Excel, select the plot line in the line chart. Press CTRL + T to play the macro you just recorded and modified.

9. Close Microsoft Excel, saving changes to the Lilliputian500 file.

EXERCISE 7.6: EMBEDDING AND LINKING OBJECTS IN EXCEL

Estimated completion time: 15 minutes

An employee at Contoso has been told to embed, not link objects in her Office documents. She doesn't understand the difference and has asked you to demonstrate how they behave differently.

1. From the Start menu, select All Programs, Microsoft Office, and select Microsoft Office Word 2003.

2. In Microsoft Word, in Document1, type **This data does not represent the Lilliputian Stock Exchange (LPSE) performance as a whole, nor is it an indicator of future performance of any part of the LPSE.**

3. From the File menu, select Save. In the Save As dialog box, navigate to Shared Documents\Lab Manual\Lab 7. In the File Name text box, type **Disclaimer**. Click Save. Close Word.

4. From the Start menu, select My Recent Documents and select Lilliputian500. In the Excel message box warning about macro security, click OK.

5. In Excel, from the Tools menu, select Options.

6. In the Options dialog box, in the Security tab, in the Macro Security section, click Macro Security.

7. In the Security dialog box, select Medium, as shown below. Click OK to close the Security dialog box. Click OK to close the Options dialog box.

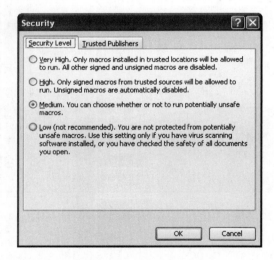

8. Close the Lilliputian500 worksheet.

9. From the Start menu, select My Recent Documents and select Lilliputian500.

10. In the Security Warning message box, click Enable Macros.

11. In the Lilliputian500 worksheet, click cell D4.

12. From the Insert menu, select Object.

13. In the Object dialog box, in the Create From File tab, select the Link To File check box. Click Browse.

14. In the Browse dialog box, navigate to Shared Documents\Lab Manual\ Lab 7. Select Disclaimer and click Insert.

15. In the Object dialog box, click OK.

16. In the Lilliputian500 worksheet, click cell D7.

17. From the Insert menu, select Object.

18. In the Object dialog box, in the Create From File tab, ensure that the Link To File check box is cleared, and click Browse.

19. In the Browse dialog box, select Disclaimer and click Insert.

20. In the Object dialog box, click OK.

21. From the Start menu, select My Recent Documents and select Disclaimer.

22. In the very beginning of the text, type **Warning:**. The text should now read:

    Warning: This data does not represent the Lilliputian Stock Exchange (LPSE) as a whole, nor is it an indicator of future performance of any part of the LPSE.

23. Press CTRL + S to save the Disclaimer document.

24. On the taskbar, click Microsoft Excel – Lilliputian500.

    QUESTION   What is the difference between the text inserted with the Link To File check box selected?

25. Close all open windows, saving the changes to the Lilliputian500 worksheet.

EXERCISE 7.7: OPENING AND REPAIRING AN OFFICE FILE

Estimated completion time: 5 minutes

You have received a corrupted Word document from an employee. You need to repair the document.

1. From the Start menu, select All Programs, Microsoft Office, and select Microsoft Office Word 2003.

2. In Word, from the File menu, select Open.

3. In the Open dialog box, navigate to Shared Documents\Lab Manual\ Lab 7.QW

4. Select Disclaimer, but do not click Open. Instead, click the small, downward-pointing triangle on the Open button, as shown below. Select Open And Repair.

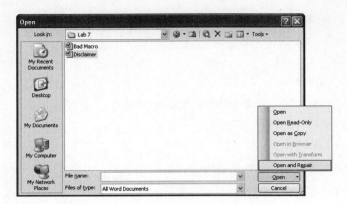

5. Close Word.

EXERCISE 7.8: USING MICROSOFT OFFICE APPLICATION RECOVERY

Estimated completion time: 15 minutes

An employee was using Word with a macro given to her by a friend. Unfortunately, the macro has caused Word to stop responding. You need to recover the application enough to save her data.

1. Log on with your student account.

2. From the Start menu, select All Programs, Microsoft Office, and select Microsoft Office Word 2003.

3. From the Tools menu, select Options.

4. In the Options dialog box, in the Security tab, in the Macro Security section, click Macro Security.

5. In the Security dialog box, in the Security Level tab, select Medium. Click OK.

6. In the Options dialog box, click OK.

7. From the File menu, select Open.

8. In the Open dialog box, navigate to Shared Documents\Lab Manual\Lab 7. Select Bad Macro and click Open.

9. In the Security Warning message box, click Enable Macros.

10. In the Bad Macro document, after Text:, type some text and press ENTER.

11. From the Tools menu, select Macro and select Macros.

12. In the Macros dialog box, ensure that BadMacro appears in the Macro Name text box, and click Run.

13. Word will stop responding.

14. Press CTRL + ESC to open the Start menu. Select All Programs, select Microsoft Office, select Microsoft Office Tools, and select Microsoft Office Application Recovery.

15. In the Microsoft Office Application Recovery dialog box, ensure that in the Application section Microsoft Office Word is selected, and click Recover Application.

16. In the Microsoft Office Word message box, click Don't Send.

17. A Microsoft Office Word message box appears and indicates the progress of recovering your document. After this, Word is launched automatically.

18. In the Security Warning dialog box, click Disable Macros.

19. The Bad Macro document should appear with the text you added plus the line "Microsoft Word will now stop responding." On the left, the Document Recovery toolbar has automatically opened.

20. In the Document Recovery pane, in the Available Files section, click the small, downward-pointing arrow on the Bad Macro [Recovered] button and select Save As.

21. In the Save As dialog box, in the File Name text box, type **Lab7-Recovered**. Click Save.

22. Close Word.

23. E-mail the Lab7-Recovered file to Instructor@contoso.com, with the subject line Student*xx*, *Your Name*, Lab 7-2, where Student*xx* is your student account user name.

EXERCISE 7.9: CONFIGURING BACKUP AND RECOVERY SETTINGS

Estimated completion time: 5 minutes

An employee has lost a number of files when Word stops responding. He wants Word configured to be aggressive in document preservation.

1. Log on with your Test account.

2. From the Start menu, select All Programs, Microsoft Office, and select Microsoft Office Word 2003.

3. In Word, from the Tools menu, select Options.

4. In the Options dialog box, in the Save tab, under Save Options, select the Always Create Backup Copy check box.

5. Next to the Save AutoRecover Info Every check box, in the Minutes text box, type **1**, as shown below. Click OK.

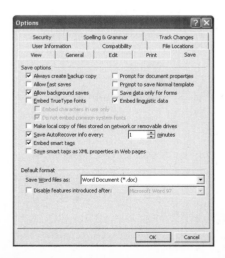

6. In the Document1 document, type some text, and wait at least one minute.

7. From the Start menu, select My Computer.

8. In the My Computer window, from the Tools menu, select Folder Options.

9. In the Folder Options dialog box, in the View tab, in the Advanced Settings list, under Hidden Files And Folders, select Show Hidden Files And Folders. Click OK. Navigate to the folder C:\Documents and Settings\Test\Application Data\Microsoft\Word.

10. From the View menu, select Refresh. Note the AutoRecovery Save Of Document1.asd file (as shown below). This is the file that would be used if AutoRecovery were performed. Close all open windows, and save changes to Document1.

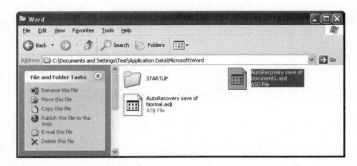

11. Close Word and do not save changes.

EXERCISE 7-10: SUBMITTING YOUR WORK

Estimated completion time: 5 minutes

The following exercise allows you to submit the work you completed in this lab to your instructor.

1. Log on with your student account.

2. E-mail the Student*xx*-Lab 7 WordPad document as an attachment to Instructor@contoso.com with the subject line Student*xx*-Lab 7 *Your Name*, where Student*xx* is your student account user name.

LAB REVIEW QUESTIONS

Estimated completion time: 15 minutes

1. Will removing an Office application by choosing the Install On First Use option remove a reference to it in the Microsoft Office programs group on the Start menu?

2. By default, what will macro security in the Microsoft Office System do with a document that contains macros?

3. What application in Microsoft Office Tools is useful in recovering data in an Office application that has stopped responding?

4. By default, how often does the Microsoft Office System save a file for AutoRecovery?

5. Where are AutoRecovery documents for Word stored?

LAB CHALLENGE: LINKING AND EMBEDDING OBJECTS IN POWERPOINT

Estimated completion time: 25 minutes

You need to assist the marketing group at Contoso in creating a Microsoft Office PowerPoint 2003 document. The PowerPoint document needs to contain charts from the Lilliputian500 file. Each slide in the document needs to contain 10 years of the price history of the Lilliputian500 Industrial Index in the form of a chart.

The charts should be created in Excel. Each chart should contain three moving-average trendlines with periods of 6, 12, and 18 months. One linear trendline should also be added. In order to automate the adding of these trendlines, you need to record a macro that adds them to an existing chart. These charts should be linked into a PowerPoint document. Make sure you do not embed the charts, as they need to change when the data in the Excel file changes.

To increase data safety, you should also configure PowerPoint to save an AutoRecovery document every minute.

REVIEWING YOUR ENVIRONMENT

You have just been promoted to be primary technical support for a new, small satellite office of Contoso, an insurance company. The office will have 15 employees sharing a total of 10 computers, 5 of which have not been set up. All of the computers will run Microsoft Windows XP Professional. The office works independently of other departments and therefore its network is not connected electronically to the Contoso domain.

The Microsoft Office System has been installed on all of the systems that are already set up. You need to configure the five computers not yet set up and add them to the network. You must configure all of the systems with multiple accounts for security reasons, and because some of the employees will be sharing computers.

After the computers are up and running, you will likely be confronted with problems associated with the following:

- Windows XP configuration
- Microsoft Outlook 2003 and e-mail delivery
- Microsoft Internet Explorer
- Installation and configuration of software
- Microsoft Office applications

Based on the information provided above and in Labs 3 through 7, answer the following questions:

1. What type of network will you use, a workgroup or a domain, and why?

2. From what dialog box in Internet Explorer do you make almost all configuration changes?

3. If a user accesses his e-mail from both his computer at home and his computer at work, how can you ensure that he will get all his e-mails at both locations?

4. If you are concerned that cookies are a security threat, what is the easiest and most thorough way to ensure that the threat is averted?

5. In Microsoft Word, where can you change the location of files used by Word?

6. What minimum level of built-in user account is necessary for installing the Microsoft Office System?

7. How do you access the Accessibility options in Internet Explorer?

LAB DEPENDENCIES

To complete this lab, you need to have completed the following:

- Lab 1, Exercises 1-1, 1-2, and 1-5
- Lab 4, Exercises 4-1 and 4-2
- Lab 6, Exercise 6-3

CHANGING THE COMPUTER CONFIGURATION

In this portion of the lab, your classmates or your instructor will change the computer configuration to create problems to troubleshoot in the next section. Three break scenarios are presented. Your instructor will decide which computers will be subject to which break scenarios.

TROUBLESHOOTING

In this portion of the lab, you must resolve problems created in the "Changing the Computer Configuration" section.

Break Scenario 1

You are the primary technical support for all users at a satellite office of Contoso Insurance. Maria Hammond, a graphic designer, reports several problems with her computer. For convenience, pretend that your student account is Maria Hammond's user account.

Her first problem is that when she opens a folder, a new window opens with it. She often ends up with 10 or more windows open on her desktop. She would like folders to open in the active window, rather than a new window.

Second, she cannot move the taskbar from the bottom of the screen to the top.

Finally, she can receive e-mails in Outlook, but receives an error message when she tries to send e-mail.

Steps for Diagnosing the Problems

1. Verify that each folder opened from My Documents is displayed in a new window rather than the current active window.

2. Verify that when you hover the mouse over the leading edge of the taskbar, the mouse cursor does not change to a resizing icon.

3. In Outlook, navigate to the E-Mail Accounts wizard on the Internet E-Mail Settings (POP3) page for the problem e-mail account, and click Test Account Settings. Read the error message.

Problem Diagnosis

1. The Browse Folder option in the Folder Options dialog box has been changed to Open Each Folder In Its Own Window.

2. The Lock The Taskbar option has been selected in the shortcut menu for the taskbar.

3. The Outgoing Mail Server (SMTP) setting in the E-Mail Accounts wizard for the problem e-mail account has been entered incorrectly.

Steps to Repair the Problems

1. Change the Browse Folders option in the General tab of the Folder Options dialog box from Open Each Folder In Its Own Window to Open Each Folder In The Same Window.

2. From the taskbar shortcut menu, clear the Lock The Taskbar option.

3. In the E-Mail Accounts wizard for the problem e-mail account, type **Server** in the Outgoing Mail Server (SMTP) text box.

Break Scenario 2

You are the primary technical support for all users at a satellite office of Contoso Insurance. Maria Hammond, a graphic designer, reports several problems with her computer. For convenience, pretend that your student account is Maria Hammond's user account.

Her first problem is that she copied her favorites from her home computer to her work computer, but they do not display when she clicks Favorites in Internet Explorer.

Second, when she is previewing the new Web site she is creating for the intranet, the fonts are not resizing according to her specifications in Hypertext Markup Language (HTML) in Internet Explorer, but are too large instead. However, they are resizing correctly in other browsers.

Finally, she visited a Web site last week that had some clip art she liked, but she cannot remember its URL and it is not showing up in her browser History.

Steps for Diagnosing the Problems

1. Click Favorites on the standard toolbar in Internet Explorer and see if her favorites are displayed. Find out to where on her work computer she copied her favorites from her home computer.

2. Go to a known site, such as *www.microsoft.com*, and see if the fonts are oversized.

3. Sort the History list in Internet Explorer by date and see how far back it goes.

Problem Diagnosis

1. Her favorites are in the wrong location. The shortcuts need to be copied from where they are to the Favorites system folder for her account.

2. The Accessibility options in Internet Explorer are set to Ignore Font Size Specifications in Web documents. Also, the text size is set to largest.

3. History of Web sites visited in Internet Explorer is set to last only for two days.

Steps to Repair the Configuration

1. Move the shortcuts in the Favorites folder she copied to My Documents to C:\Documents and Settings\student*xx*\Favorites, where student*xx* is your student account user name.

2. In Internet Explorer, in the Accessibility dialog box, clear the Ignore Font Sizes Specified On Web Pages check box. From the View menu, select Text Size and select Medium.

3. In Internet Explorer, in the Internet Options dialog box, in the General tab, enter **20** in the Days To Keep Pages In History text box.

Break Scenario 3

You are the primary technical support for all users at a satellite office of Contoso Insurance. Maria Hammond, a graphic designer, reports several problems with Word. For convenience, pretend that your student account is Maria Hammond's user account.

She says that when she uses Word, "There are a bunch of extra characters, like backwards Ps." She reports that the extra characters do not show up when she prints.

Second, when she types **Contoso**, and runs the spelling checker, Word wants to correct it to "Contoso."

Finally, she pasted a bitmap image in BMP format in her document, but the image stopped showing up. She reorganized her My Pictures folder before the image stopped displaying in Word.

Steps for Diagnosing the Problems

1. Start Word and type some text. Verify that there are "extra characters."

2. Start Word and type both **Contoso** and **Cnotoso**. Run the spelling checker.

3. Open the document (Project.doc) that she is having trouble with and see if the picture displays. In the View tab of the Options dialog box, select the Field Codes check box in the Show section. Note the path that is specified for the picture.

Problem Diagnosis

1. Word is configured to display formatting marks.

2. A custom entry for "Contoso" in the dictionary was accidentally mis-spelled "Cnotoso."

3. The BMP file was moved and the link no longer points to the correct loca-tion, which is indicated in the field code.

Steps to Repair the Configuration

1. In Word, clear the All check box in the View tab of the Options dialog box in the Formatting Marks section 2. In Word, remove the entry in the custom dictionary for "Cnotoso" and add an entry for "Contoso."

2. Either reinsert the picture as a link to the new location, using the Link To File option accessed from the Insert button in the Insert Picture dialog box, or move the picture to the path specified in the field code for the link.

LAB 8

CONFIGURING AND TROUBLESHOOTING CONNECTIVITY

This lab contains the following exercises and activities, some of which are optional:

- Exercise 8.1: Configuring an Internet Connection
- Exercise 8.2: Installing a Modem (Optional)
- Exercise 8.3: Querying a Modem from Modem Properties (Optional)
- Exercise 8.4: Common Modem Settings (Optional)
- Exercise 8.5: Changing Workgroups
- Exercise 8.6: Using the Repair Feature for Network Connections
- Exercise 8.7: Obtaining an Automatic Private IP Address
- Exercise 8.8: Joining a Domain
- Exercise 8.9: Using Network Diagnostics in the Help and Support Center
- Exercise 8.10: Using PING
- Exercise 8.11: Using Tracert, Pathping, and NSlookup
- Exercise 8.12: Restoring the System for Future Labs
- Exercise 8.13: Submitting Your Work
- Exercise 8.14: Installing Microsoft ActiveSync (Optional)
- Exercise 8.15: Setting up a Partnership and Synchronizing a Pocket PC (Optional)
- Exercise 8.16: Dealing with Synchronization Conflicts (Optional)
- Lab Review Questions
- Lab Challenge 8.1: Using the Command Line to Troubleshoot a Connection Failure
- Lab Challenge 8.2: Synchronization Preferences

BEFORE YOU BEGIN

If you have not installed and configured Microsoft Office Outlook 2003 according to Lab 4, Exercises 4.1 and 4.2, or according to the "Before You Begin" section of Labs 5, 6, or 7, you must complete those exercises before you can complete this lab.

SCENARIO

You are a technical support agent at Contoso, an insurance provider. Recently, many new employees have been added to the network and given limited Internet access. It is your job to troubleshoot the network and Internet connectivity.

After completing this lab, you will be able to:

- Install and configure a dial-up connection
- Change workgroups
- Use and understand the Repair feature for network connections
- Use APIPA
- Join a computer to a domain
- Use Network Diagnostics in the Help And Support Center
- Use command-line utilities to diagnose network problems

Estimated lesson time: 100 minutes

Estimated lesson time for optional exercises: 70 minutes

> **NOTE**   Exercises 8-1 and 8-2 configure a connection and modem that will not be functional. They are only installed to allow practice with their user interfaces.

EXERCISE 8.1: CONFIGURING AN INTERNET CONNECTION

Estimated completion time: 5 minutes

An executive of Contoso brings in his laptop computer and wants you to configure his computer for dial-up connectivity.

1. Log on with your administrator account (the password is P@ssw0rd).

2. From the Start menu, select My Network Places.

3. In the My Network Places window, in the Network Tasks section, click View Network Connections.

4. In the Network Connections window, in the Network Tasks section, click Create A New Connection.

5. In the New Connection Wizard, on the Welcome To The New Connection Wizard page, click Next.

6. On the Network Connection Type page, verify that Connect To The Internet is selected and click Next.

7. On the Getting Ready page, select Set Up My Connection Manually, and click Next.

8. On the Internet Connection page, verify that Connect Using A Dial-Up Modem is selected, and click Next.

9. On the Connection Name page, in the ISP Name text box, type **Contoso**, and click Next.

10. On the Phone Number To Dial page, in the Phone Number text box, type **1-000-000-0000**. Click Next.

11. On the Internet Account Information page, in the User Name text box, type your name. In the Password and Confirm Password text boxes, type **P@ssw0rd**. Click Next.

12. On the Completing The New Connection Wizard page, click Finish.

   QUESTION   Why might you see a red X over the Contoso connection icon in the Network Connections window?

   NOTE   Because this lab is long, the following exercise is optional. It can be skipped without consequence to future labs. However, if you do not complete this exercise, you should not complete Exercises 8-3 or 8-4.

EXERCISE 8.2: INSTALLING A MODEM (OPTIONAL)

Estimated completion time: 10 minutes

Now that you have created an Internet connection for the executive in the previous exercise, you need to install a modem.

1. In Control Panel (switch to Classic view if necessary), double-click Add Hardware.

2. In the Add Hardware Wizard, on the Welcome To The Add Hardware Wizard page, click Next.

3. On the Is The Hardware Connected? page, select Yes, I Have Already Connected The Hardware, and click Next.

4. On the The Following Hardware Is Already Installed On Your Computer page, in the Installed Hardware list, scroll to the bottom and select Add A New Hardware Device, as shown below. Click Next.

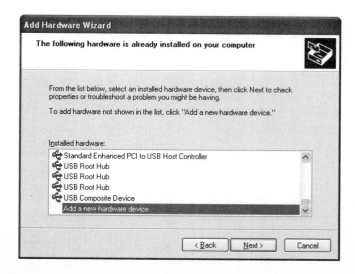

5. On the The Wizard Can Help You Install Other Hardware page, select Install The Hardware That I Manually Select From A List (Advanced), and click Next.

6. On the From The List Below, Select The Type Of Hardware You Are Installing page, in the Common Hardware Types list box, select Modems. Click Next.

7. On the Install New Modem page, select the Don't Detect My Modem; I Will Select It From A List check box, and click Next.

8. On the Install New Modem page, in the Manufacturer list box, ensure that (Standard Modem Types) is selected. In the Models list box, select Standard 56000 bps Modem and click Next.

9. On the Install New Modem page, in the ports window, select COM1. Click Next.

10. The Install New Modem page appears. Click Finish when it becomes active.

11. Close all open windows.

12. From the Start menu, select My Network Places.

13. In the My Network Places window, under Network Tasks, select View Network Connections.

14. Take a snapshot of the Network Connections window and paste it into a WordPad document called Student*xx*-Lab 8, where Student*xx* is your student account user name, and save the file in Shared Documents\Lab Manual\Lab 8.

> **QUESTION**   If you saw a red X on the Contoso connection previously, why has the icon changed?

> **NOTE**   Because this lab is long, the following exercise is optional. It can be skipped without consequence to future labs. However, if you do not complete this exercise, you should not complete Exercise 8-4.

EXERCISE 8.3: QUERYING A MODEM FROM MODEM PROPERTIES (OPTIONAL)

Estimated completion time: 5 minutes

To see if the executive's modem is communicating with the computer, you will query it for information in the following steps.

1. From the Start menu, right-click My Computer and select Manage.

2. In the Computer Management console, in the console tree, expand System Tools and select Device Manager.

3. In the details pane, under the COMPUTERXX node, expand Modems, as shown below. Right-click Standard 56000 bps Modem and select Properties.

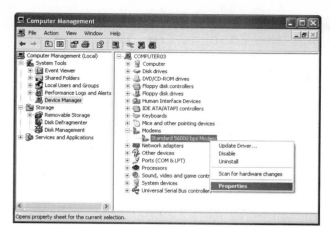

4. In the Standard 56000 bps Modem Properties dialog box, in the Diagnostics tab, click Query Modem.

5. In the Error message box, click OK. Below is depicted an example of what a correctly configured modem produces when queried in this manner. Close all open windows.

QUESTION   Why is querying the modem from the Modem Properties dialog box a good diagnostic measure when probing connectivity problems with a modem?

NOTE   Because this lab is long, the following exercise is optional. It can be skipped without consequence to future labs.

EXERCISE 8.4: COMMON MODEM SETTINGS (OPTIONAL)

Estimated completion time: 5 minutes

The modem from the previous exercise is now working, but you want to fine-tune the settings according the user's preferences.

Turning Off the Speaker and Enabling Error Correction and Flow Control

The following steps will turn off the speaker, and change settings that might improve a faulty connection.

1. Log on with your administrator account (the password is P@ssw0rd).

2. From the Start menu, select My Network Places.

3. In the My Network Places window, in the Network Tasks section, click View Network Connections.

4. In the Network Connections window, under Dial-Up, right-click Contoso and select Properties.

5. In the Contoso Properties dialog box, in the General tab, click Configure.

6. In the Modem Configuration dialog box, clear the Enable Modem Speaker check box.

   NOTE Hardware error correction and flow control can sometimes improve the performance of a line with a lot of noise or other problems. If a user is making a connection, but that connection is unreliable, try enabling these options.

7. If necessary, select the Enable Hardware Flow Control and Enable Modem Error Control check boxes, as shown below. Click OK.

Disabling Hang-up When Idle

The network connection from the modem is working great, with one exception: if it is left idle for too long, it disconnects.

1. In the Contoso Properties, select the Options tab.

2. Under Redialing Options, in the Idle Time Before Hanging Up drop-down list, select Never. Click OK.

3. Close the Network Connections window.

EXERCISE 8.5: CHANGING WORKGROUPS

Estimated completion time: 15 minutes

A small division of Contoso uses workgroups instead of joining to the Contoso domain. The workgroup is getting too large, though, and needs to be divided into two groups.

1. From the Start menu, select My Network Places.

2. In the My Network Places window, in the Network Tasks section, click View Workgroup Computers.

3. Note the computers present in the workgroup.

4. From the Start menu, select Run.

5. In the Run dialog box, type **cmd** and press ENTER.

6. At the command line, type **ipconfig** and press ENTER. Copy your IP address here: _____.

7. At the command line, type **exit** and press ENTER.

8. From the Start menu, right-click My Computer and select Properties.

9. In the System Properties dialog box, in the Computer Name tab, click Change.

10. In the Computer Name Changes dialog box, under Member Of, in the Workgroup text box, enter the following:

    ❑ If your IP address ends with an odd number, type **ODDCOMPUTERS**.

    ❑ If your IP address ends with an even number, type **EVENCOMPUTERS**.

11. Click OK.

12. In the Computer Name Changes message box welcoming you to the new workgroup, click OK.

13. In the Computer Name Changes message box instructing you to restart to activate changes, click OK.

14. In the System Properties dialog box, click OK.

15. In the System Settings Change message box, asking if you want to restart your computer, click Yes.

16. Log on with your administrator account.

17. From the Start menu, select My Network Places.

18. In My Network Places, in the Network Tasks section, click View Workgroup Computers.

19. Note that half of the computers have been removed, and the title of the window has changed.

> **QUESTION**   Are the other half of the computers in the classroom unavailable to you?

20. From the Start menu, select Run.

21. In the Run dialog box, in the Open text box, type **10.1.1.**_xx_, where _xx_ is the last octet of your IP address minus one. However, if the last octet of your IP address is 1, type **10.1.1.2**. Press ENTER.

> **NOTE**   Example: If your address is 10.1.1.32, type **10.1.1.31** in the Open text box and press ENTER.

22. Note that you have access to non-workgroup computers.

EXERCISE 8.6: USING THE REPAIR FEATURE FOR NETWORK CONNECTIONS

Estimated completion time: 10 minutes

When a user at Contoso loses connectivity, it is standard procedure to run a repair on the connection, which is outlined in the following steps.

1. From the Start menu, select My Network Places.

2. In the My Network Places window, in the Network Tasks section, select View Network Connections.

3. In the Network Connections window, under LAN Or High-Speed Internet, right-click Local Area Connection and select Repair.

4. In the Repair Connection message box, click OK.

> **NOTE**   When a Repair command is issued, the following are executed:
>
> ❑ Dynamic Host Configuration Protocol (DHCP) lease is renewed: **ipconfig /renew**
>
> ❑ Address Resolution Protocol (ARP) cache is flushed: **arp -d**
>
> ❑ Reload of the NetBIOS name cache: **nbtstat -R**
>
> ❑ NetBIOS name update is sent: **nbtstat -RR**
>
> ❑ Domain Name System (DNS) cache is flushed: **ipconfig /flushdns**
>
> ❑ DNS name registration: **ipconfig /registerdns**
>
> ❑ For Windows XP Service Pack 1: **IEEE 802.1X Authentication Restart**
>
> The following steps manually re-create the actions of the Repair option.

5. Minimize the Network Connections window. Click OK in the Repair Connection message box.

6. Open a Command Prompt window.

7. At the command prompt, type **ipconfig /release** and press ENTER.

8. At the command prompt, type **ipconfig /renew** and press ENTER.

9. At the command prompt, type **arp -d** and press ENTER.

10. At the command prompt, type **nbtstat -R** and press ENTER.

11. At the command prompt, type **nbtstat -RR**, and press ENTER.

12. At the command prompt, type **ipconfig /flushdns** and press ENTER.

13. At the command prompt, type **ipconfig /registerdns** and press ENTER. An example of all these commands being run is shown below.

14. At the command prompt, type **exit** and press ENTER.

15. From the taskbar, restore the Network Connections window.

16. Right-click Local Area Connection and select Properties.

17. In the Local Area Connection Properties dialog box, in the Authentication tab, clear the Enable IEEE 802.1x Authentication For This Network check box. Click OK.

18. Right-click Local Area Connection and select Properties.

19. In the Local Area Connection Properties dialog box, in the Authentication tab, select the Enable IEEE 802.1x Authentication For This Network check box. Click OK.

NOTE Steps 17 through 19 are a re-creation of the last step that the Repair button executes: IEEE 802.1X Authentication Restart.

EXERCISE 8.7: OBTAINING AN AUTOMATIC PRIVATE IP ADDRESS

Estimated completion time: 5 minutes

A DHCP server that serves workgroup computers has gone down. Until the problem is fixed, the IT department has decided to use Automatic Private IP Addressing (APIPA) because the number of computers on the network is small.

1. Log on with your administrator account (the password is P@ssw0rd).

2. From the Start menu, select Run.

3. In the Run dialog box, in the Open text box, type **cmd** and press ENTER.

4. At the command prompt, type **ipconfig /release** and press ENTER.

5. At the command prompt, type **ipconfig /renew** and press ENTER.

6. At the command prompt, type **ipconfig /all** and press ENTER.

> **QUESTION**   What is the new IP address?

> **QUESTION**   To complete this exercise, the classroom scope on the DHCP server was deactivated. Once the DHCP server is fully activated again, what is the least action you can take to obtain a DHCP address instead of an APIPA address?

> **NOTE**   Your instructor will now reactivate the DHCP scope for the classroom, so that you can obtain a DHCP IP address.

7. At the command prompt, type **ipconfig /release** and press ENTER.

8. At the command prompt, type **ipconfig /renew** and press ENTER.

EXERCISE 8.8: JOINING A DOMAIN

Estimated completion time: 10 minutes

Employees previously isolated from the Contoso domain in a workgroup need to have their computers added to the domain.

1. From the Start menu, right-click My Computer and select Properties.

2. In the System Properties dialog box, in the Computer Name tab, click Change.

3. In the Computer Name Changes dialog box, in the Member Of section, select Domain. In the Domain text box, type **contoso** and press ENTER.

4. In the Computer Name Changes dialog box, in the User Name text box, type **AddToDomain**, and in the Password text box, type **P@ssw0rd,** as shown below. Click OK.

5. In the Computer Name Changes message box welcoming you to the Contoso domain, click OK.

6. In the Computer Name Changes message box instructing you to restart your computer, click OK.

7. In the System Properties dialog box, click OK.

8. In the System Settings Change message box, click Yes to answer that you want to restart.

9. In the Welcome To Windows message box, press CTRL + ALT + DELETE.

10. In the Log On To Windows dialog box, click Options.

11. In the Log On To drop-down list, select CONTOSO.

12. In the User name box, type **Student*xx***, where **Student*xx*** is the name of your student account user name. In the Password text box, type **P@ssw0rd**. Click OK.

13. From the Start menu, select Run. In the Run dialog box, in the Open text box, type **cmd** and press ENTER.

14. At the command prompt, type **net config workstation** and press ENTER.

15. Take a snapshot of the command prompt window, an example of which is shown below, and paste it into the Student*xx*-Lab8 WordPad document that you created earlier.

```
C:\WINDOWS\System32\cmd.exe                                           _ □ ×
Microsoft Windows XP [Version 5.1.2600]
(C) Copyright 1985-2001 Microsoft Corp.

C:\Documents and Settings\Student03.CONTOSO>net config workstation
Computer name                          \\COMPUTER03
Full Computer name                     computer03.contoso.com
User name                              Student03

Workstation active on
        NetbiosSmb (000000000000)
        NetBT_Tcpip_{ACC26EA0-2DF8-4983-BA2D-6687078C6580} (00E04CEDFA1F)

Software version                       Windows 2002

Workstation domain                     CONTOSO
Workstation Domain DNS Name            contoso.com
Logon domain                           CONTOSO

COM Open Timeout (sec)                 0
COM Send Count (byte)                  16
COM Send Timeout (msec)                250
The command completed successfully.

C:\Documents and Settings\Student03.CONTOSO>
```

16. Close all open windows.

EXERCISE 8.9: USING NETWORK DIAGNOSTICS IN THE HELP AND SUPPORT CENTER

Estimated completion time: 10 minutes

You are having trouble diagnosing a problem with the network. A Tier 2 technician has asked you to produce a diagnostic report on the networking components of the computer.

1. Log on to the Contoso domain with your student account (the password is P@ssw0rd).

2. Click the desktop in a blank area and press F1 to start the Help And Support Center.

3. In the Help And Support Center, in the Search text box, type **diagnose network**, and press ENTER.

4. In the Search Results pane, under Pick A Task, select Diagnose Network Configuration And Run Automated Networking Tests.

5. On the Network Diagnostics page, click Set Scanning Options.

6. Under Options, select and clear the check boxes as shown below.

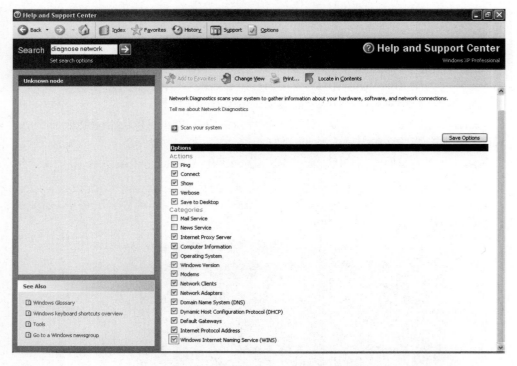

7. Once the options are set, click Scan Your System. The more computers that are on the network, the longer the scan will take.

   QUESTION   What three broad categories are the results of the scan divided into?

   QUESTION   What is the default gateway according to the results of the diagnosis?

8. On the Network Diagnostics page, click Save To File. This will place a file on the desktop that can be used for diagnosing network problems. It contains the results of the scan.

9. In the VBScript message box, click OK.

10. Log off and log on to your local administrator account (the password is P@ssw0rd).

11. From the Start menu, select My Network Places.

12. In the My Network Places window, in the Network Tasks section, click View Network Connections.

13. In the Network Connections window, under LAN Or High-Speed Internet, right-click Local Area Connection and select Disable.

14. Click a blank space in the Network Connections window.

15. In the See Also section, click Network Troubleshooter.

16. In the Help And Support Center, on the Networking Problems page, under Fix A Problem, click Diagnose Network Configuration And Run Automated Networking Tests.

17. On the Network Diagnostics page, click Set Scanning Options. Set the options according to step 6. Click Scan Your System. Note that many of the diagnostics are different because the network card has been disabled. Example results are shown below.

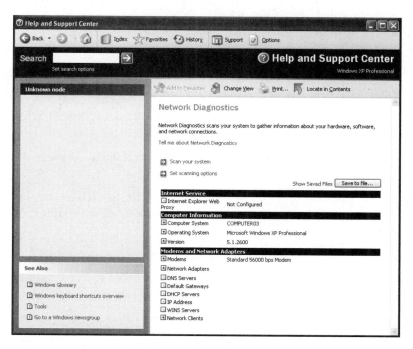

18. In the Network Connections window, right-click Local Area Connection and select Enable.

19. Close all open windows.

EXERCISE 8.10: USING PING

Estimated completion time: 10 minutes

To solve common networking issues, you use several command-line tools. A user has had a network diagnostics and a repair run on her computer but still has connectivity problems. It is your task to use command-line tools to help diagnose the problem.

The following steps use the Ping command to check connectivity.

1. Log on with your local administrator account (the password is P@ssw0rd).

2. From the Start menu, select Run. In the Run dialog box, in the Open text box, type **cmd** and press ENTER.

3. At the command prompt, type **ping 127.0.0.1** and press ENTER. A sample result is shown below.

4. Minimize the command prompt window.

5. From the Start menu, select My Network Places.

6. In the My Network Places window, in the Network Tasks section, click View Network Connections.

7. In the Network Connections window, right-click Local Area Connection and select Properties.

8. In the Local Area Connection Properties dialog box, in the General tab, in the This Connection Uses The Following Items section, clear the Internet Protocol (TCP/IP) check box and click OK.

9. In the Network Connections message box, click Yes.

10. Minimize the Network Connections window, and restore the command prompt window.

11. At the command prompt, type **ping 127.0.0.1** and press ENTER.

12. At the command prompt, type **ping -n 20 computer*xx***, where **computer*xx*** is the number of a computer next to you that is attached to the classroom network. Press ENTER.

13. Minimize the command prompt window and restore the Network Connections window.

14. In the Network Connections window, under LAN Or High-Speed Internet, right-click Local Area Connection and select Properties.

15. In the Local Area Connection Properties dialog box, in the General tab, in the This Connection Uses The Following Items section, select the Internet Protocol (TCP/IP) check box, as shown below, and click OK.

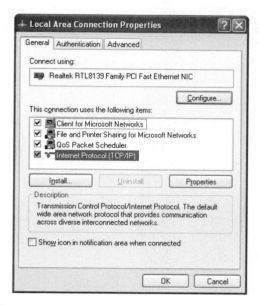

16. Close the Network Connections window and restore the command prompt window.

> **NOTE**   Before you complete step 17, be sure that the computer you are pinging has completed up to and including step 15.

17. Press the up arrow key to restore the previous command and press ENTER.

EXERCISE 8.11: USING TRACERT, PATHPING, AND NSLOOKUP

Estimated completion time: 10 minutes

After investigating connectivity in the previous exercise with Ping, you need to use other command-line tools to try to figure out the problem.

Using Pathping

The following steps use the Pathping command to diagnose connectivity.

1. From the Start menu, select Run. In the Run dialog box, in the Open text box, type **cmd** and press ENTER.

2. In the command prompt window, type **pathping www.microsoft.com** and press ENTER. Sample results from this command are shown below.

3. Take a few moments to note what statistics Pathping gathers.

Using Tracert

The following steps use the Tracert command, which is similar to Pathping.

1. At the command prompt, type **tracert www.microsoft.com** and press ENTER.

2. Compare the information relayed by Tracert with that of Pathping.

Using NSlookup

The following steps purge your DNS cache and query available DNS servers.

1. At the command prompt, type **ipconfig /flushdns** and press ENTER.

2. At the command prompt, type **nslookup www.microsoft.com** and press ENTER.

QUESTION   What information does the NSlookup command convey in this instance?

EXERCISE 8.12: RESTORING THE SYSTEM FOR FUTURE LABS

Estimated completion time: 5 minutes

This exercise must be finished to make Lab 8 compatible with subsequent labs. It will remove the modem that you installed so that it won't interfere with exercises on network connections.

1. Log on with your local administrator account (the password is P@ssw0rd).

2. From the Start menu, select My Network Places.

3. In the My Network Places window, in the Network Tasks section, select View Network Connections.

4. In the Network Connections window, under Dial-Up, right-click Contoso and select Delete.

5. In the Confirm Connection Deletion message box, click Yes. Close the Network Connections window.

6. From the Start menu, right-click My Computer and select Properties.

7. In the System Properties dialog box, in the Hardware tab, in the Device Manager section, click Device Manager.

8. In Device Manager, expand the Modems node. Right-click Standard 56000 bps Modem and select Uninstall. Click OK to confirm that you want to uninstall the modem.

9. Close Device Manager and close the System Properties dialog box.

EXERCISE 8.13: SUBMITTING YOUR WORK

Estimated completion time: 5 minutes
This exercise allows you to submit the work you completed in this lab to your instructor.

1. Log on with your student account.

2. E-mail the Student*xx*-Lab 8 WordPad document as an attachment to Instructor@contoso.com with the subject line Student*xx*-Lab 8 *Your Name*, where Student*xx* is your student account user name.

> **NOTE** Because this lab is long, the following exercise is optional. It can be skipped without consequence to future labs. However, if you do not complete this exercise, you should not complete Exercises 8-15 or 8-16.

EXERCISE 8.14: INSTALLING MICROSOFT ACTIVESYNC (OPTIONAL)

Estimated completion time: 15 minutes
Many employees that travel have recently been given Pocket PCs. You will need to assist these employees in using these devices.

The following steps will install Microsoft ActiveSync 3.7.1.

1. Log on with your local administrator account (the password is P@ssw0rd).

2. From the Start menu, select Internet Explorer.

3. In Internet Explorer, in the Address text box, ensure that **http:// www.microsoft.com** is entered.

4. On the Microsoft home page, in the Resources section on the left, click Downloads.

5. On the Download Center page, in the Search For A Download section, in the Product/Technology drop-down list, select ActiveSync. Click Go.

6. In the Search Results list, click ActiveSync 3.7.1 (if you cannot find this through the search just described, go to *http://www.microsoft.com/ downloads/details.aspx?FamilyID=2eb5bd80-d52c-4560-ae11- da92f2b229fa&DisplayLang=en*).

7. On the Microsoft ActiveSync 3.7.1 page, click Download.

8. In the File Download dialog box, click Save.

9. In the Save As dialog box, click the My Documents icon on the left, and click Save.

10. In the Download Complete dialog box, click Open.

11. Close Internet Explorer.

12. In the Microsoft ActiveSync wizard, on the Set Up Microsoft ActiveSync 3.7.1 page, click Next.

13. On the Select Installation Folder page, click Next.

14. On the Get Connected page, as seen below, follow the on-screen instructions and click Next.

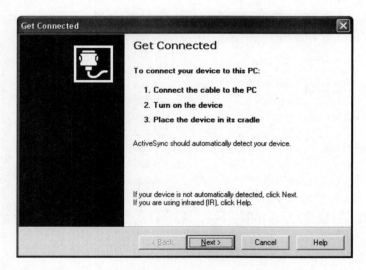

15. In the New Partnership wizard, click Cancel.

16. In the Partnership Not Set Up message box, click OK.

17. Close Microsoft ActiveSync.

NOTE Because this lab is long, the following exercise is optional. It can be skipped without consequence to future labs. However, if you do not complete this exercise, you should not complete Exercise 8-16.

EXERCISE 8.15: SETTING UP A PARTNERSHIP AND SYNCHRONIZING A POCKET PC (OPTIONAL)

Estimated completion time: 15 minutes

The following steps will configure a partnership between your computer and Pocket PC and demonstrate synchronization of Outlook contacts.

1. Log on with your local student account.

2. From the Start menu, select E-Mail. Select the Outlook profile if asked.

3. In Outlook, from the Go menu, select Contacts.

4. In Contacts – Microsoft Outlook, on the Standard toolbar, click New.

5. In the Untitled – Contact dialog box, in the Full Name text box, type **Your Name**, as shown below. Then, on the Standard toolbar, click Save And Close.

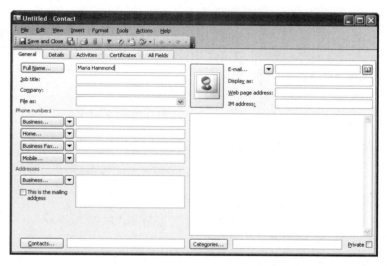

6. Close Microsoft Outlook.

7. Turn on your Pocket PC and insert it into its cradle (the cradle should be plugged into a USB port and have power).

8. From the Start menu, select All Programs and then select Microsoft ActiveSync.

9. In the New Partnership wizard, on the Set Up A Partnership page, click Next.

10. On the Specify How To Synchronize Data page, ensure that Synchronize With This Desktop Computer is selected. Click Next.

11. On the Select Number Of Partnerships page, click Next.

12. On the Select Synchronization Settings page, click Next to accept the default synchronization settings.

13. On the Setup Complete page, click Finish. The Synchronization phase will start. You might be asked which profile to use. Select Outlook.

14. Once synchronization is complete, remove your Pocket PC from its cradle.

15. On your Pocket PC, tap Start and then tap Contacts. Note that your name has been added to the Contacts list. Tap and hold on your name in the Contacts list and then select Delete Contact.

16. In the Contacts message box, tap Yes. Close the Contacts window.

17. Replace the Pocket PC into its cradle. Synchronization should automatically start. If asked, select the Outlook profile.

18. Once synchronization is complete, from the Start menu, select E-Mail. If asked, select the Outlook profile.

19. In Microsoft Outlook, from the Go menu, select Contacts. Note that your name has been removed from the Contacts list.

20. Close all open windows.

> **NOTE** Because this lab is long, the following exercise is optional. It can be skipped without consequence to future labs.

EXERCISE 8.16: DEALING WITH SYNCHRONIZATION CONFLICTS (OPTIONAL)

Estimated completion time: 20 minutes
The following steps will create and resolve a synchronization conflict.

1. Remove your Pocket PC from its cradle.

2. From the Start menu, select All Programs and select Microsoft ActiveSync.

3. In Microsoft ActiveSync, from the Tools menu, select Options.

4. In the Options dialog box, in the Sync Options tab, in the Mobile Device list, select the Files check box, as shown below.

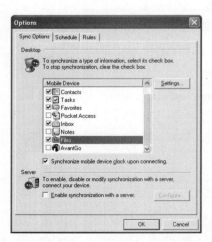

5. In the File Synchronization message box, click OK.

6. In the Options dialog box, click OK. Close Microsoft ActiveSync.

7. From the Start menu, select My Documents.

8. In My Documents, open the Pocket_PC My Documents Folder.

9. From the File menu, select New and select Text Document. Type **Sample** for the name and press ENTER.

10. Open the Sample text document.

11. In the Sample – Notepad window, type the following, as shown below:

    line 1

    line 2

    line 3

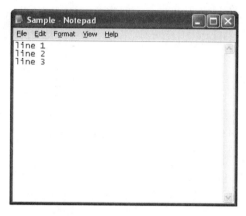

12. From the File menu, select Save.

13. From the File menu, select Exit.

14. Minimize the Pocket_PC My Documents folder.

15. Insert your Pocket PC into its cradle.

16. Remove your Pocket PC from its cradle.

17. Restore the Pocket_PC My Documents folder from the taskbar.

18. Open the Sample text document.

19. Replace the first line (line 1) with **Change on computer**.

20. From the File menu, select Save.

21. From the File menu, select Exit.

22. On your Pocket PC, from the Start menu, select Programs.

23. In the Programs window, tap File Explorer.

24. In the File Explorer window, in the My Documents page, tap Sample.

25. Replace the second line (line 2) with **Change on Pocket PC**. Click OK to close and save the Sample text document. Close the File Explorer window. Close the Programs window.

26. Replace your Pocket PC in its cradle. Synchronization should start automatically. If asked, select the Outlook profile.

27. Microsoft ActiveSync reports that there is one unresolved item.

28. In Microsoft ActiveSync, click Resolve Items.

29. In the Resolve Conflict dialog box, in the Action drop-down list, select the left-pointing Replace arrow, as shown below. Click Synchronize.

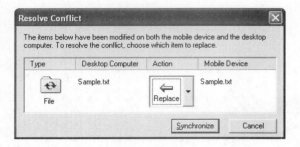

QUESTION   Which version of the Sample.txt document will both your computer and Pocket PC contain?

LAB REVIEW QUESTIONS

Estimated completion time: 15 minutes

1. Where can you find out what COM port a modem is configured to use?

2. How do you change workgroups?

3. Can a computer in a domain access the shared resources of another computer on the network that is not a member of the domain?

4. List the tasks that a network connection repair involves.

5. What command-line utility reports on data loss and the route to a particular IP address?

6. What will the -n switch do when used with the Ping command?

7. What Microsoft utility is commonly used to synchronize mobile devices with desktop computers?

8. By default, when conflicting versions of a file are synchronized between a desktop computer and a mobile device using Microsoft ActiveSync, which copy of the file replaces the other?

9. What items on a Pocket PC are by default selected for synchronization?

LAB CHALLENGE 8.1: USING THE COMMAND LINE TO TROUBLESHOOT A CONNECTION FAILURE

Estimated completion time: 10 minutes

You are a technical support agent at Contoso.com. A user complains that she cannot access a site on the Internet. In investigating the problem, you ask her several questions:

■ Are you able to access any other site on the Internet? Yes.

■ Have you ever accessed this site before? Yes, but not on this computer.

■ Was the computer on the same network, or on a different network? It was at home.

■ Have you made any changes recently to Microsoft Internet Explorer or your computer? No.

■ What is the site? *www.dell.com*

Try to access *www.dell.com* from your computer (you will be unable). Using the tools presented in this lab, rule out your network card and DNS as the culprit. Find out at which IP address the failure is occurring.

LAB CHALLENGE 8.2: SYNCHRONIZATION PREFERENCES

Estimated completion time: 15 minutes

An employee at Contoso has a Pocket PC and would like to customize its synchronizations with his desktop computer.

First, he travels frequently and would like his Pocket PC to maintain the time he sets it to, rather than having it change according to his computer's time. Second, he takes notes on his Pocket PC in the Notes application. He would like these notes automatically copied to his computer. Third, he wants to start the synchronizations manually, rather than having it occur automatically. Finally, he would like the items changed on the Pocket PC to always override changes made on his computer. After you have completed these changes, you need to test them.

LAB 9

SECURITY AND SHARING IN WINDOWS XP PROFESSIONAL

This lab contains the following exercises and activities:

- Exercise 9.1: Sharing a Document Locally
- Exercise 9.2: Sharing Folders in a Workgroup Using Simple File Sharing
- Exercise 9.3: Making a Folder Private
- Exercise 9.4: Sharing Folders in a Workgroup Without Simple File Sharing
- Exercise 9.5: Setting NTFS Permissions on a Shared Network Folder
- Exercise 9.6: Adding a User to the Backup Operators Group
- Exercise 9.7: Setting Password Policies
- Exercise 9.8: Setting Lockout Policies
- Exercise 9.9: Assigning User Rights
- Exercise 9.10: Configuring Security Options
- Exercise 9.11: Configuring Group Policy in a Workgroup
- Lab Review Questions
- Lab Challenge: Determining Resultant User Rights

BEFORE YOU BEGIN

If you have completed Lab 8, Exercise 8.5 or 8.8, you need to complete the following exercise to return your computer to the workgroup WORKGROUP.

Adding Your Computer to the Correct Workgroup

Estimated completion time: 5 minutes

The following steps will add your computer to the workgroup WORKGROUP.

1. Log on locally with your administrator account (the password is P@ssw0rd).

2. From the Start menu, right-click My Computer and select Properties.

3. In the System Properties dialog box, in the Computer Name tab, click Change.

4. In the Computer Name Changes dialog box, in the Member Of section, select Workgroup. In the Workgroup text box, type **WORKGROUP**. Click OK.

5. In the Computer Name Changes dialog box, in the User Name text box, type **AddToDomain**. In the Password text box, type **P@ssw0rd**. Click OK.

6. In the Computer Name Changes message box welcoming you to the workgroup, click OK.

7. In the Computer Name Changes message box telling you to restart, click OK.

8. In the System Properties dialog box, click OK.

9. In the System Settings Change message box, click Yes to restart your computer.

If you have not installed and configured Microsoft Office Outlook 2003 according to Lab 4, Exercises 4-1 and 4-2, or according to the Before You Begin section of Lab 5, 6, 7, or 8, you must complete those exercises before you can complete this lab.

SCENARIO

You are a technical support agent at Contoso, a provider of insurance. Recently, many new employees have been added to the network and it is your job to make changes to file sharing and security settings to accommodate the new users.

After completing this lab, you will be able to:

- Share documents locally and on a network
- Make a folder private
- Set NTFS permissions for folders
- Add users to groups
- Set password and lockout policies
- Assign user rights
- Configure security options
- Configure group policies

Estimated lesson time: 85 minutes

EXERCISE 9.1: SHARING A DOCUMENT LOCALLY

Estimated completion time: 5 minutes

A user has created a collaborative scheduling document that all users of the computer need to be able to update. You need to share the document locally so that all local users can have full access to it.

1. Log on with your student account.

2. Right-click the desktop, select New, and select Text Document. Type **Shared Document** for the name of the document and press ENTER.

3. Right-click Shared Document on the desktop and select Cut.

4. From the Start menu, select My Computer.

5. In the My Computer window, open the Shared Documents folder.

6. In the Shared Documents folder, from the Edit menu, select Paste.

QUESTION   Will placing a file or folder in the Shared Documents folder share it on the network?

EXERCISE 9.2: SHARING FOLDERS IN A WORKGROUP USING SIMPLE FILE SHARING

Estimated completion time: 10 minutes

A financial analyst for Contoso has produced accounting documents that he needs to be able to share over the network.

1. Log on with your student account.

2. From the Start menu, select My Documents.

3. In My Documents, from the File menu, select New and select Folder.

4. Type **Cash Flow Projections for 2005** for the name of the folder and press ENTER.

5. Right-click the newly created folder and select Sharing And Security.

QUESTION   Why can't you share the folder?

6. Log off and log back on with your administrator account (the password is P@ssw0rd).

7. From the Start menu, select My Computer.

8. In My Computer, navigate to the following folder: C:\Documents and Settings\Student*xx*\Student*xx*'s Documents, where Student*xx* is your student account user name.

9. In the Student*xx*'s Documents folder, right-click the Cash Flow Projections For 2005 folder and select Sharing And Security.

10. In the Cash Flow Projections For 2005 Properties dialog box, in the Sharing tab, in the Network Sharing And Security section, select the Share This Folder On The Network check box. Also select the Allow Network Users To Change My Files check box, as shown below. Click OK.

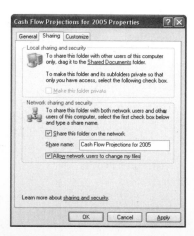

11. In the Sharing message box, click Yes.

12. From the Start menu, select My Network Places.

13. In My Network Places, from the View menu, select Refresh. Note the folders that your classmates have shared.

EXERCISE 9.3: MAKING A FOLDER PRIVATE

Estimated completion time: 5 minutes

After sharing his documents, the accountant from Exercise 9-2 finds that he wants to make some changes before anybody else can access the documents.

1. Log on with your student account.

2. From the Start menu, select My Documents.

3. In My Documents, right-click Cash Flow Projections For 2005 and select Properties.

4. In the Cash Flow Projections For 2005 Properties dialog box, in the Sharing tab, in the Local Sharing And Security section, select the Make This Folder Private check box. Click OK.

5. In the Sharing message box, click No.

6. Log off and log back on with your administrator account (the password is P@ssw0rd).

7. From the Start menu, select My Computer.

8. In My Computer, under Files Stored On This Computer, open Student*xx*'s Documents, where Student*xx* is your student account user name.

9. In Student*xx*'s Documents, double-click Cash Flow Projections For 2005.

   QUESTION   What occurs when you try to open this folder?

10. Close all open windows.

EXERCISE 9.4: SHARING FOLDERS IN A WORKGROUP WITHOUT SIMPLE FILE SHARING

Estimated completion time: 10 minutes

A network administrator has some how-to technical documents that she wants shared on the network. However, she wants access to be restricted to administrators only.

1. Log on with your administrator account (the password is P@ssw0rd).

2. From the Start menu, select My Computer.

3. In My Computer, from the Tools menu, select Folder Options.

4. In the Folder Options dialog box, in the View tab, in the Advanced Settings window, scroll to the end and clear the Use Simple File Sharing (Recommended) check box. Click OK.

5. In My Computer, open the Administrator's Documents Folder.

6. In My Documents, from the File menu, select New and select Folder.

7. Type **Administrator's Share** for the name of the folder and press ENTER.

8. Right-click Administrator's Share and select Sharing And Security.

9. In the Administrator's Share Properties dialog box, select Share This Folder. Click Permissions.

10. In the Permissions For Administrator's Share dialog box, ensure that Everyone is selected in the Group Or User Names window. Click Remove. Click Add.

11. In the Select Users Or Groups dialog box, click Advanced.

12. In the second Select Users Or Groups dialog box, click Find Now.

13. In the search pane, select Administrators and click OK.

14. In the first Select Users Or Groups dialog box, click OK.

15. In the Permissions For Administrator's Share dialog box, under Permissions For Administrators, select the Change check box in the Allow column, as shown below. Click OK.

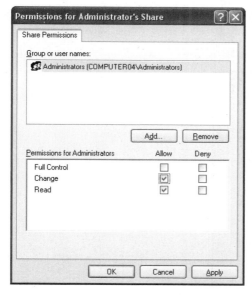

16. In the Administrator's Share Properties dialog box, click OK.

17. In My Documents, under Other Places on the left, click My Network Places.

18. In My Network Places, from the View menu, select Refresh.

19. Open a folder named Administrator's Share On Computer*xx*, where Computer*xx* is *not* your computer name.

20. Log off and log back on with your student account.

21. From the Start menu, select My Network Places.

22. Double-click a folder named Administrator's Share On Computer*xx*, where Computer*xx* is *not* your computer name.

   QUESTION   *Why are you unable to open the folder?*

EXERCISE 9.5: SETTING NTFS PERMISSIONS ON A SHARED NETWORK FOLDER

Estimated completion time: 10 minutes

The administrator from Exercise 9-4 decides that the contents of the folder she shared could be educational to all users, and now wants it shared on the network for everyone.

1. Log on with your administrator account (the password is P@ssw0rd).

2. From the Start menu, select My Documents.

3. In My Documents, right-click the Administrator's Share folder and select Properties.

4. In the Administrator's Share Properties dialog box, in the Sharing tab, click Permissions.

5. In the Permissions dialog box, click Add.

6. In the Select Users Or Groups dialog box, in the Enter The Object Name To Select text box, type **Everyone**. Click Check Names. Click OK.

7. In the Permissions For Administrator's Share dialog box, in the Permissions For Everyone section, select the Change check box in the Allow column, as shown below. Click OK.

8. In the Administrator's Share Properties dialog box, in the Security tab, click Add.

9. In the Select Users Or Groups dialog box, in the Enter The Object Name To Select text box, type **Everyone**. Click Check Names. Click OK.

10. In the Administrator's Share Properties dialog box, in the Security tab, select the Write check box in the Deny column, as shown below. Click Advanced.

NOTE *Steps 11 and 12 do not set or change any settings, but exist only to demonstrate how NTFS permissions work.*

11. In the Advanced Security Settings For Administrator's Share dialog box, in the Permissions Entries list box, select Read And Execute in the Permission column. Click Edit. The Permission Entry For Administrator's Share dialog box appears, as shown below. This dialog box shows the low-level NTFS permissions that constitute the Read And Execute permission.

12. In the Permission Entry For Administrator's Share dialog box, click Cancel.

13. In the Advanced Security Settings For Administrator's Share dialog box, click OK.

14. In the Administrator's Share Properties dialog box, click OK.

15. In the Security message box, click Yes.

16. Log off and log back on with your student account.

17. From the Start menu, select My Network Places.

18. Double-click a folder named Administrator's Share On Computer*xx*, where Computer*xx* is *not* your computer name.

QUESTION *Why are you now able to access the shared folder when you weren't able to before?*

19. Close all open windows.

EXERCISE 9.6: ADDING A USER TO THE BACKUP OPERATORS GROUP

Estimated completion time: 5 minutes

A secretary is responsible for maintaining his boss's calling list and other important data. He likes to be very safe with this information and wants to be able to back it up daily and control the backup parameters himself. After discussing with him the responsibilities and security issues involved, you decide to make him a backup operator.

1. Log on with your administrator account (the password is P@ssw0rd).

2. From the Start menu, right-click My Computer and select Manage.

3. In the Computer Management console, in the console tree, expand System Tools, expand Local Users And Groups, and select Users.

4. In the details pane, right-click Student*xx*, where Student*xx* is your Student account user name, and select Properties.

5. In the Student*xx* Properties dialog box, in the Member Of tab, click Add.

6. In the Select Groups dialog box, click Advanced.

7. In the second Select Groups dialog box, click Find Now.

8. In the search pane, select Backup Operators and click OK.

9. In the Select Groups dialog box, click OK.

10. In the Student*xx* Properties dialog box, click OK.

11. Close the Computer Management console.

EXERCISE 9.7: SETTING PASSWORD POLICIES

Estimated completion time: 10 minutes

You have been asked to demonstrate to new Tier 1 technical support agents how to change password policies.

1. Log on with your administrator account (the password is P@ssw0rd).

2. From the Start menu, select Control Panel.

3. In Control Panel, ensure that you are using Classic view, and double-click Administrative Tools.

4. In the Administrative Tools window, double-click Local Security Policy.

5. In the Local Security Settings console, expand Account Policies, and select Password Policy, as shown below.

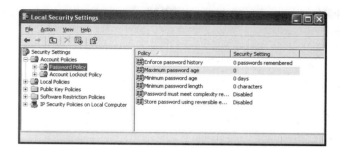

NOTE *Each of the password policies can be set by double-clicking on the policy name in the details pane.*

6. In the details pane, double-click Maximum Password Age.

7. In the Maximum Password Age Properties dialog box, in the Password Will Expire In text box, enter **0**. Click OK.

8. Close all open windows.

EXERCISE 9.8: SETTING LOCKOUT POLICIES

Estimated completion time: 10 minutes

To guard against hackers or employees attempting to guess the password of an account that does not belong to them, you need to implement an account lockout policy.

1. From the Start menu, select Control Panel.

2. In Control Panel, ensure that you are using Classic view, and double-click Administrative Tools.

3. In the Administrative Tools window, double-click Local Security Policy.

4. In the Local Security Settings console, expand Account Policies, and select Account Lockout Policy.

5. In the details pane, double-click Account Lockout Threshold.

6. In the Account Lockout Threshold Properties dialog box, in the Account Will Lock Out After: text box, enter **5**, as shown below. Click OK.

7. In the Suggested Value Changes dialog box, click OK.

8. Log off, and log back on with your Test account but use the incorrect password X. Do this five times. Eventually, the Log On To Windows dialog box will be grayed out.

9. Press CTRL + ALT + DELETE. A message box explaining that you have been locked out will appear.

10. Try logging on with the correct password (the correct password is nothing). You will not be able to log on.

11. Log on with your administrator account (the password is P@ssw0rd).

12. From the Start menu, select Control Panel.

13. In Control Panel, ensure that you are using Classic view, and double-click Administrative Tools.

14. In the Administrative Tools window, double-click Computer Management.

15. In the Computer Management console, in the console tree, expand System Tools, expand Local Users And Groups, and select Users.

16. In the details pane, right-click Test and select Properties.

17. In the Test Properties dialog box, in the General tab, clear the Account Is Locked Out check box, as shown below, and click OK.

18. Close all open windows.

EXERCISE 9.9: ASSIGNING USER RIGHTS

Estimated completion time: 5 minutes

A user has a system clock that is inaccurate and drifts a few minutes each week. Rather than resetting the clock yourself once a week, you decide to give the user the right to set the system time himself.

1. Log on with your administrator account (the password is P@ssw0rd).

2. From the Start menu, select Control Panel.

3. In Control Panel, ensure that you are using Classic view, and double-click Administrative Tools.

4. In the Administrative Tools window, double-click Local Security Policy.

5. In the Local Security Settings console, expand Local Policies, and select User Rights Assignment.

6. In the details pane, right-click Change The System Time and select Properties.

7. In the Change The System Time Properties dialog box, click Add User Or Group.

8. In the Select Users Or Groups dialog box, in the Enter The Object Names To Select (Examples) text box, type **Student*xx***, where **Student*xx*** is your student account user name. Click Check Names and then click OK.

9. In the Change The System Time Properties dialog box, click OK.

10. Close all open windows.

EXERCISE 9.10: CONFIGURING SECURITY OPTIONS

Estimated completion time: 5 minutes

A user broke her wrist and can type with only one hand. She finds it difficult to press CTRL + ALT + DELETE when logging on. You need to disable the security option that requires this.

1. From the Start menu, select Control Panel.

2. In Control Panel, ensure that you are using Classic view, and double-click Administrative Tools.

3. In the Administrative Tools window, double-click Local Security Policy.

4. In the Local Security Settings console, expand Local Policies, and select Security Options.

5. In the details pane, right-click Interactive Logon: Do Not Require CTRL + ALT + DEL, and select Properties, as shown below.

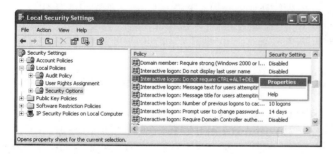

6. In the Interactive Logon: Do Not Require CTRL + ALT + DEL Properties dialog box, select Enabled and click OK.

7. Close all open windows.

EXERCISE 9.11: CONFIGURING GROUP POLICY IN A WORKGROUP

Estimated completion time: 5 minutes

You have set the properties for the Recycle Bin as you want them, and you want to prevent users from accessing the Properties option from the Recycle Bin's shortcut menu.

1. From the Start menu, select Run.

2. In the Run dialog box, in the Open text box, type **gpedit.msc** and press ENTER.

3. In the Group Policy console, in the console tree, expand User Configuration, expand Administrative Templates, and select Desktop.

4. In the details pane, right-click Remove Properties From The Recycle Bin Context Menu, and select Properties.

5. In the Remove Properties From The Recycle Bin Context Menu Properties dialog box, select Enabled and click OK.

6. Close all open windows and right-click the Recycle Bin. Note that Properties is no longer an option on the shortcut menu.

LAB REVIEW QUESTIONS

Estimated completion time: 15 minutes

1. When you make a folder private locally, and the folder is shared over a workgroup network, is the folder available to remote users?

2. How do you prevent users from changing files in a folder shared on the network in simple file sharing?

3. What is the effect of denying an NTFS permission for a group, when a member of that group is a member of multiple groups and is allowed the same NTFS permission in a different group?

4. After completing Exercise 9-5, if you were to log on as an administrator, and tried to create a new file in the Administrator's Share folder from another student's computer, what would happen? How would it differ if you did the same thing but logged on with your student account?

LAB CHALLENGE: DETERMINING RESULTANT USER RIGHTS

Estimated completion time: 20 minutes

Your supervisor wants to adjust the rights assignments of the built-in groups. First, however, he wants to know what rights are assigned to what groups. You need to list all the rights assigned on your computer to the following groups:

■ Administrators

■ Power Users

- Users

- Backup Operators

Once you are done, compile the list into a text document and e-mail it to Instructor@ contoso.com, with the subject line **Student***xx,* ***Your Name***, **Lab 9-Challenge**, where Student*xx* is your student account user name.

LAB 10

UPDATING AND PROTECTING WINDOWS XP PROFESSIONAL

This lab contains the following exercises and activities:

■ Exercise 10.1: Manually Updating Windows

■ Exercise 10.2: Enabling ICF

■ Exercise 10.3: Enabling an ICMP Component

■ Exercise 10.4: Logging with ICF

■ Exercise 10.5: Starting a Service within ICF

■ Exercise 10.6: Removing ICF

■ Exercise 10.7: Installing MBSA

■ Exercise 10.8: Using MBSA

■ Exercise 10.9: Submitting Your Work

■ Lab Review Questions

■ Lab Challenge: Automating Windows Update

BEFORE YOU BEGIN

If you have completed Lab 8, Exercise 8.5 or 8.8, you need to complete the following exercise to return your computer to the workgroup WORKGROUP.

Adding Your Computer to the Correct Workgroup

Estimated completion time: 5 minutes

The following steps will add your computer to the workgroup WORKGROUP.

1. Log on locally with your administrator account (the password is P@ssw0rd).

2. From the Start menu, right-click My Computer and select Properties.

3. In the System Properties dialog box, in the Computer Name tab, click Change.

4. In the Computer Name Changes dialog box, in the Member Of section, select Workgroup. In the Workgroup text box, type **WORKGROUP**. Click OK.

5. In the Computer Name Changes dialog box, in the User Name text box, type **AddToDomain**. In the Password text box, type **P@ssw0rd**. Click OK.

6. In the Computer Name Changes message box welcoming you to the workgroup, click OK.

7. In the Computer Name Changes message box telling you to restart, click OK.

8. In the System Properties dialog box, click OK.

9. In the System Settings Change message box, click Yes to restart your computer.

If you have not installed and configured Microsoft Office Outlook 2003 according to Lab 4, Exercises 4-1 and 4-2, or according to the Before You Begin section of Lab 5, 6, 7, 8, or 9, you must complete those exercises before you can complete this lab.

SCENARIO

You are a technical support agent at Contoso, a provider of insurance. Recently, many of the systems have been upgraded to Windows XP Professional, and it is your job to ensure that the installations are up to date and protected.

After completing this lab, you will be able to:

- **Use Windows Update**
- **Use Internet Connection Firewall (ICF)**
- **Enable Internet Control Message Protocol (ICMP) components for diagnostic purposes**
- **Use ICF to log connectivity events**
- **Start a service within ICF**
- **Install and use Microsoft Baseline Security Analyzer (MBSA)**

Estimated lesson time: 95 minutes

EXERCISE 10.1: MANUALLY UPDATING WINDOWS

Estimated completion time: 20 minutes
You have received a bulletin from your supervisor that you need to install some updates immediately to deal with imminent security threats.

1. Log on with your administrator account (the password is P@ssw0rd).

2. From the Start menu, right-click My Computer and select Properties.

3. In the System Properties dialog box, in the Automatic Updates tab, clear the Keep My Computer Up To Date. With This Setting Enabled, Windows

Update Software May Be Automatically Updated Prior To Applying Any Other Updates check box, as seen below. Click OK.

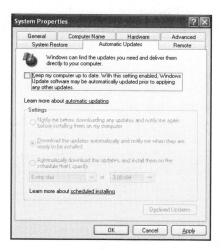

4. From the Start menu, select All Programs and select Internet Explorer.

5. In Internet Explorer, in the Address text box, type **http://www. windowsupdate.com** and press ENTER.

6. In the Security Warning dialog box, click Yes to install Windows Update.

7. The Windows Update site spends some time checking for updates. When it finishes, on the Welcome To Windows Update page, click Scan For Updates.

8. In the Windows Update section on the left, expand Pick Updates To Install, and click Critical Updates And Service Packs. An example list of available critical updates and service packs is shown below.

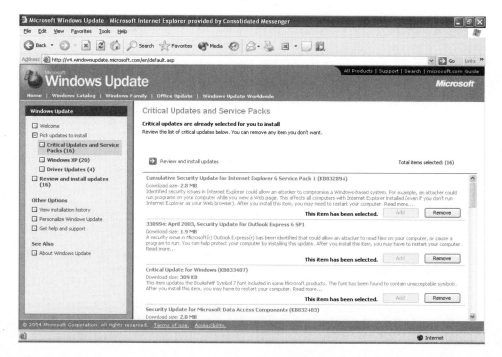

9. On the Critical Updates And Service Packs page, click Review And Install Updates.

10. Click Remove next to all the updates except for one less than 500 K. For classroom purposes, the smaller the remaining update, the better. Click Install Now.

11. A Windows Update dialog box appears and displays progress. Once installation is complete, you might receive a Microsoft Internet Explorer message box asking if you want to restart the computer. If so, click OK (if the computer does not restart automatically, restart it manually). Once the computer restarts, log on with your administrator account.

12. Complete steps 4, 5, and 7 of this exercise again, and then continue with step 13.

13. On the Pick Updates To Install page, in the Windows Update section on the left, click Windows XP.

14. On the Windows XP Updates page, click Add for the smallest update available. Click Review And Install Updates.

QUESTION   On the Total Selected Updates page, what updates has Windows Update automatically added?

15. Remove all the updates except for the one you manually selected, which will be the last in the list. Click Install Now.

16. A Windows Update dialog box appears and displays progress. Once installation is complete, you might receive an Internet Explorer message box asking if you want to restart the computer. If so, click OK (if the computer does not restart automatically, restart it manually). When the computer restarts, log on with your administrator account.

17. Complete steps 4 and 5 of this exercise again, and then continue with step 18.

18. On the Welcome To Windows Update page, in the Windows Update section on the left, under Other Options, click View Installation History. Take a screen shot of the active window displaying the installation history and paste it into a WordPad document called Student*xx*-Lab10, where Student*xx* is your student account user name. Save the document in the Shared Documents folder.

19. Close all open windows.

EXERCISE 10.2: ENABLING ICF

Estimated completion time: 5 minutes
An executive at Contoso often works at home, and you need to secure his home network by installing an ICF.

NOTE   Ordinarily, you would not install ICF on a computer that is not connected directly to the Internet. However, for the purpose of practice, this exercise has you install ICF. Be certain that if you complete this exercise, you also complete Exercise 10-6, which removes ICF.

This exercise requires a partner. You will need your partner's Internet Protocol (IP) address. Your IP address can be determined by running Ipconfig at the command line.

1. From the Start menu, select My Network Places.

2. In My Network Places, in the Network Tasks section on the left, click View Network Connections.

3. In the Network Connections window, right-click Local Area Connection and select Properties.

4. In the Local Area Connection Properties dialog box, in the Advanced tab, in the Internet Connection Firewall section, select the Protect My Computer And Network By Limiting Or Preventing Access To This Computer From The Internet check box. Click OK.

   NOTE Wait until your partner has completed step 4 and then continue.

5. From the Start menu, select Run.

6. In the Run dialog box, in the Open text box, type **cmd** and press ENTER.

7. At the command prompt, type **ping 10.1.1.*xx***, where 10.1.1.*xx* is the IP address of your partner's computer.

   QUESTION Why did your partner's computer not respond to the Ping command?

8. Close all open windows.

EXERCISE 10.3: ENABLING AN ICMP COMPONENT

Estimated completion time: 10 minutes

To assist in troubleshooting the home network of the executive from the previous exercise, you want the ICF to allow the computer to respond to pings.

   NOTE This exercise requires a partner. You will need your partner's IP address. Your IP address can be determined by running Ipconfig at the command line.

1. From the Start menu, select My Network Places.

2. In My Network Places, in the Network Tasks section on the left, click View Network Connections.

3. In the Network Connections window, right-click Local Area Connection and select Properties.

4. In the Local Area Connection Properties dialog box, in the Advanced tab, click Settings.

5. In the Advanced Settings dialog box, in the ICMP tab, select the Allow Incoming Echo Request check box. Click OK.

6. In the Local Area Connection Properties dialog box, click OK.

   NOTE Wait until your partner has completed step 6 and then continue.

7. From the Start menu, select Run.

8. In the Run dialog box, in the Open text box, type **cmd** and press ENTER.

9. At the command prompt, type **ping 10.1.1.*xx***, where 10.1.1.*xx* is the IP address of your partner's computer.

10. Close all open windows.

EXERCISE 10.4: LOGGING WITH ICF

Estimated completion time: 15 minutes

You fear that a computer connected directly to the Internet at work is being attacked. The computer is running ICF. You need to enable logging to see if you can record any unwanted network activity.

> **NOTE**   This exercise requires a partner. You will need your partner's IP address. Your IP address can be determined by running Ipconfig at the command line.

1. From the Start menu, select My Network Places.

2. In My Network Places, in the Network Tasks section on the left, click View Network Connections.

3. In the Network Connections window, right-click Local Area Connection and select Properties.

4. In the Local Area Connection Properties dialog box, in the Advanced tab, click Settings.

5. In the Advanced Settings dialog box, in the Security Logging tab, in the Logging Options section, select the Log Dropped Packets check box.

6. In the Advanced Settings dialog box, in the ICMP tab, ensure that all check boxes are cleared, as shown below. Click OK.

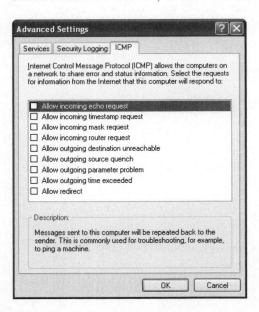

7. In the Local Area Connection Properties dialog box, click OK.

8. Close the Network Connections window.

9. From the Start menu, select Run.

10. In the Run dialog box, in the Open text box, type **cmd** and press ENTER.

    NOTE   *Wait until your partner has completed step 10 and then continue.*

11. At the command prompt, type **ping 10.1.1.*xx***, where 10.1.1.*xx* is the IP address of your partner's computer. The Ping command will fail.

    NOTE   *Wait until your partner has completed step 11 and then continue.*

12. From the Start menu, select My Computer.

13. In My Computer, double-click Local Disk (C:).

14. In the Local Disk (C:) window, if the files are hidden, in the System Tasks section, click Show The Contents Of This Drive. Open the Windows folder.

15. In the Windows folder, if the files are hidden, in the System Tasks section, click Show The Contents Of This Folder. Locate the log file Pfirewall and double-click it. What you see will be similar to the example below.

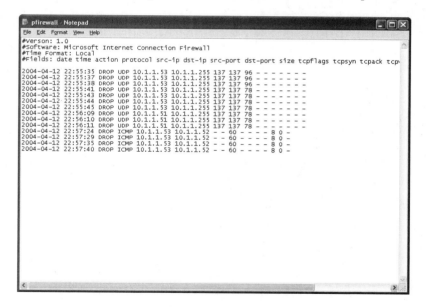

    QUESTION   *How can you tell which packets were dropped as a result of the Ping command that your partner performed on your IP address?*

16. Close all open windows.

EXERCISE 10.5: STARTING A SERVICE WITHIN ICF

Estimated completion time: 5 minutes

To provide support to a remote home user running ICF, you want to be able to use remote desktop. You need to enable the service that allows remote desktop to work with ICF.

1. From the Start menu, select My Network Places.

2. In My Network Places, in the Network Tasks section on the left, click View Network Connections.

3. In the Network Connections window, right-click Local Area Connection and select Properties.

4. In the Local Area Connection Properties dialog box, in the Advanced tab, click Settings.

5. In the Advanced Settings dialog box, in the Services tab, select the Remote Desktop check box.

6. In the Service Settings dialog box, ensure that your computer's name is in the Name Or IP Address (For Example 192.168.0.12) Of The Computer Hosting This Service On Your Network text box, as shown below. Click OK.

7. In the Advanced Settings dialog box, click OK.

8. In the Local Area Connection Properties dialog box, click OK.

9. Close all open windows.

EXERCISE 10.6: REMOVING ICF

Estimated completion time: 5 minutes

The following steps will remove ICF from your computer, which returns connectivity in the workgroup to normal.

1. From the Start menu, select My Network Places.

2. In My Network Places, in the Network Tasks section on the left, click View Network Connections.

3. In the Network Connections window, right-click Local Area Connection and select Properties.

4. In the Local Area Connection Properties dialog box, in the Advanced tab, clear the Protect My Computer And Network By Limiting Or Preventing Access To This Computer From The Internet check box. Click OK.

5. In the Internet Connection Firewall message box, click Yes.

EXERCISE 10.7: INSTALLING MBSA

Estimated completion time: 15 minutes

Management has become more concerned with security since hackers infiltrated the company's systems last month. You have been asked to help improve security by finding weaknesses. To assist in this, you need to install and use MBSA.

The following steps will install MBSA.

1. Log on with your administrator account (the password is P@ssw0rd).

2. Copy the MBSA install file (MBSAsetup-en.msi) from the network share specified by the instructor to your My Documents folder.

3. In My Documents, double-click MBSAsetup-en.

4. In the MBSA Setup wizard, on the Welcome To The Microsoft Baseline Security Analyzer page, click Next.

5. On the License Agreement page, select I Accept The License Agreement and click Next.

6. On the Destination Folder page, click Next.

7. On the Start Installation page, click Install.

8. Close all open windows.

EXERCISE 10.8: USING MBSA

Estimated completion time: 10 minutes

The following steps will use MBSA to audit the security on multiple computers on the network.

1. From the Start menu, select All Programs and select Microsoft Baseline Security Analyzer 1.2.

2. In the Microsoft Baseline Security Analyzer wizard, on the Welcome To The Microsoft Baseline Security Analyzer page, click Scan More Than One Computer.

3. On the Pick Multiple Computers To Scan page, in the IP Address Range text boxes, enter a range covering only two IP addresses, one of which should be your IP address. An example is shown below. Click Start Scan.

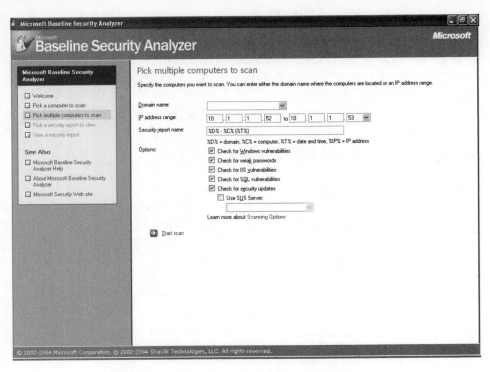

4. The Scanning page appears and indicates progress. The scanning might take 5 minutes or more.

5. On the Pick A Security Report To Review page, in the Computer Name column click Workgroup\Computer*xx*, where Computer*xx* is the name of your computer.

6. On the View Security Report screen, take a moment to browse the results. Take a screen shot of the active window and paste it into the Student*xx*-Lab10 WordPad document that you created earlier.

7. Close all open windows.

EXERCISE 10.9: SUBMITTING YOUR WORK

Estimated completion time: 5 minutes
The following exercise allows you to submit the work you completed in this lab to your instructor.

1. Log on with your student account.

2. E-mail the Student*xx*-Lab10 WordPad document as an attachment to Instructor@contoso.com with the subject line Student*xx*-Lab 10 *Your Name*, where Student*xx* is your student account user name.

LAB REVIEW QUESTIONS

Estimated completion time: 15 minutes

1. Into what three categories are Windows Updates divided?

2. What adverse effects can ICF have on diagnosing troubles in a network?

3. Suppose you were running ICF with logging, and you were trying to determine if an outside source was trying to attack your network. What would you look for in the Pfirewall Src-Ip column?

4. If you knew that your password scheme was weak, and you wanted MBSA to analyze your security minus your password scheme, what would you do?

LAB CHALLENGE: AUTOMATING WINDOWS UPDATE

Estimated completion time: 20 minutes

NOTE Depending on the speed of your Internet connection and the number of updates available, this lab challenge could take 30 minutes or more.

You have been assigned to ensure that all the company computers are protected by installing all available critical updates and service packs from Windows Update. Before doing this, you test each of the updates on a test system to ensure that none of the updates causes adverse effects.

Now you need to install all available updates on each system. After that, you need to configure each system to automatically retrieve and install updates every Thursday morning at 2 A.M.

LAB 11
MULTIUSER AND MULTIBOOT COMPUTERS

This lab contains the following exercises and activities:

- Exercise 11.1: Adding User Accounts to Multiuser Computers in a Workgroup

- Exercise 11.2: Sharing Applications on a Multiuser Computer

- Exercise 11.3: Configuring Boot Options on a Multiboot Computer

- Exercise 11.4: Configuring Program Compatibility Settings

- Exercise 11.5: Using Remote Desktop

- Lab Review Questions

- Lab Challenge: Resolving File Ownership Problems after an Upgrade to Windows XP

BEFORE YOU BEGIN

If you have completed Lab 8, Exercise 8.5 or 8.8, and have not completed the "Before You Begin" section in Lab 9 or 10, you need to complete the following exercise to return your computer to the workgroup WORKGROUP.

Adding Your Computer to the Correct Workgroup

Estimated completion time: 5 minutes

The following steps will add your computer to the workgroup WORKGROUP.

1. Log on locally with your administrator account (the password is P@ssw0rd).

2. From the Start menu, right-click My Computer and select Properties.

3. In the System Properties dialog box, in the Computer Name tab, click Change.

4. In the Computer Name Changes dialog box, in the Member Of section, select Workgroup. In the Workgroup text box, type **WORKGROUP**. Click OK.

5. In the Computer Name Changes dialog box, in the User Name text box, type **AddToDomain**. In the Password text box, type **P@ssw0rd**. Click OK.

6. In the Computer Name Changes message box welcoming you to the workgroup, click OK.

7. In the Computer Name Changes message box telling you to restart, click OK.

8. In the System Properties dialog box, click OK.

9. In the System Settings Change message box, click Yes to restart your computer.

If you have not installed and configured Microsoft Office Outlook 2003 according to Lab 4, Exercises 4.1 and 4.2, or according to the "Before You Begin" section of Lab 5, 6, 7, 8, 9, or 10, you must complete those exercises before you can complete this lab.

SCENARIO

You are a Tier 1 technical support agent serving internal clients at Contoso, an insurance company. Contoso has many multiuser computers, and therefore many multiuser support issues. A few users in the accounting department have computers that are multiboot systems so that they can run legacy software that doesn't run as smoothly under Microsoft Windows XP.

After completing this lab, you will be able to:

■ Add user accounts to workgroup computers

■ Share applications on multiuser computers

■ Configure boot options on multiboot computers

■ Set program compatibility settings

■ Use Remote Desktop

Estimated lesson time: 80 minutes

EXERCISE 11.1: ADDING USER ACCOUNTS TO MULTIUSER COMPUTERS IN A WORKGROUP

Estimated completion time: 15 minutes
A night shift has been added to your customer service department, and the new employees will be using the same computers as the day-shift employees. You need to add user accounts for the new users.

Adding a Power User Account

1. The head of the night shift is computer literate and has requested privileges that match those in the Power Users group. After discussing the security implications with the user, you agree to grant her a Power User account. Log on with your administrator account (the password is P@ssw0rd).

2. From the Start menu, right-click My Computer and select Manage.

3. In the Computer Management console, expand System Tools, expand Local Users And Groups, and select Users. From the Action menu, select New User.

4. In the New User dialog box, in the User Name text box, type **JohnD**. In the Full Name text box, type **John Doe**. In the Password and Confirm Password text boxes, type **P@ssw0rd.**

5. Clear the User Must Change Password At Next Logon check box, as shown below. Click Create. Click Close.

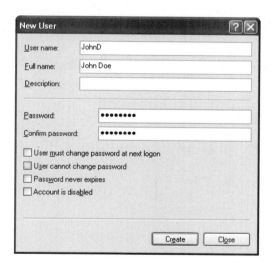

6. In the Computer Management console, in the details pane, right-click JohnD and select Properties.

7. In the JohnD Properties dialog box, in the Member Of tab, click Add.

8. In the Select Groups dialog box, in the Enter The Object Names To Select (Examples) text box, type **Power Users** and click Check Names. Click OK.

9. In the JohnD Properties dialog box, click OK.

10. Log off and log back on as JohnD (the password is P@ssw0rd).

Adding a Guest Account

To allow a frequent visitor from a partner company Internet access without granting any privileges that might compromise security, you need to create a guest account.

1. Log on with your administrator account (the password is P@ssw0rd).

2. From the Start menu, right-click My Computer and select Manage.

3. In the Computer Management console, expand System Tools, expand Local Users And Groups, and select Users. From the Action menu, select New User.

4. In the New User dialog box, in the User Name text box, type **MariaH**. Clear the User Must Change Password At Next Logon check box. Click Create. Click Close.

5. In the Computer Management console, in the details pane, right-click MariaH and select Properties.

6. In the MariaH Properties dialog box, in the Member Of tab, select Users and click Remove. Click Add.

7. In the Select Groups dialog box, in the Enter The Object Names To Select (Examples) text box, type **Guests** and click Check Names, as shown below. Click OK.

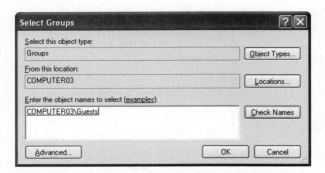

8. In the MariaH Properties dialog box, click OK.

9. Close the Computer Management console.

10. From the Start menu, select Run.

11. In the Run dialog box, in the Open text box, type **cmd** and press ENTER.

12. At the command prompt, type **net user**. Take a screen shot of the command prompt window and paste it into a WordPad document called Student*xx*-Lab11, where Student*xx* is your student account user name. Save the document in the Shared Documents folder.

EXERCISE 11.2: SHARING APPLICATIONS ON A MULTIUSER COMPUTER

Estimated completion time: 25 minutes

As an administrator, you have two user accounts. One has administrator-level access, and you use it when privileged access is necessary. For normal tasks, however, you have a user account. To increase security, you use this account when doing mundane tasks that don't require heightened access.

Sometimes, however, you need access to your user account e-mail when you are logged on as an administrator.

1. Log on with your administrator account (the password is P@ssw0rd).

2. From the Start menu, select All Programs, Microsoft Office, and select Microsoft Office Outlook 2003.

3. In the Outlook 2003 Startup window, click Next.

4. On the E-Mail Account page, verify that Yes is selected and click Next.

5. In the E-Mail Accounts wizard, on the Server Type page, select POP3 and click Next.

6. On the Internet E-Mail Settings (POP3) page, under User Information, in the Your Name box, type *Your Name*. In the E-Mail Address text box, type **studentxx@contoso.com**, where **studentxx** is your student account user name.

7. Under Server Information, in the Incoming Mail Server (POP3) and Outgoing Mail Server (SMTP) text boxes, type **Server**.

8. Under Logon Information, in the User Name text box, type **studentxx**, where **studentxx** is your student account user name. In the Password text box, type **P@ssw0rd**. An example is shown below. Click Next.

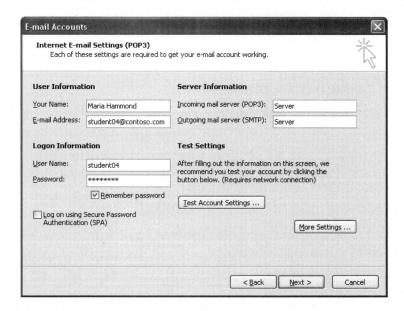

9. On the Congratulations page, click Finish.

10. In the User Name dialog box, click OK.

> **QUESTION**   *Why aren't your e-mails from your student installation of Outlook present in your administrator installation?*

11. From the Start menu, select My Computer.

12. In My Computer, from the Tools menu, select Folder Options.

13. In the Folder Options dialog box, in the View tab, in the Advanced Settings pane, under Hidden Files And Folders, select Show Hidden Files And Folders. Also in the Advanced Settings pane, clear the Hide Protected And Operating System Files (Recommended) check box. In the Warning message box, click Yes. Click OK.

14. In Outlook, from the Tools menu, select Options.

15. In the Options dialog box, in the Mail Setup tab, click E-Mail Accounts.

16. In the E-Mail Accounts wizard, click Next.

17. On the E-Mail Accounts page, click New Outlook Data File.

18. In the New Outlook Data File dialog box, click OK.

19. In the Create Or Open Outlook Data File dialog box, click the My Computer icon on the left.

20. Navigate to the location of the .pst file for your student account. It will be located in a network share if you completed Exercise 4.4. Otherwise, it will be in the folder C:\Documents and Settings\Student*xx*\Local Settings\ Application Data\Microsoft\Outlook. Select Outlook.pst and click OK.

21. In the Personal Folders dialog box, in the Name text box, type ***Your Name*** and click OK.

22. In the E-Mail Accounts wizard, on the E-Mail Accounts page, in the Deliver New E-Mail To The Following Location drop-down list, select *Your Name*. Click Finish.

23. In the Account Manager message box, click OK.

24. In the Options dialog box, click OK.

25. In Outlook, note that in the scope pane a new node named *Your Name* has been added. This new node contains the items that Outlook contains when you log on with your student account.

26. In the scope pane, right-click the Personal Folders node. Note that the Close "Personal Folders" option is unavailable.

27. Close and reopen Outlook.

28. In Outlook, in the scope pane, right-click the Personal Folders node and select Close "Personal Folders".

EXERCISE 11.3: CONFIGURING BOOT OPTIONS ON A MULTIBOOT COMPUTER

Estimated completion time: 5 minutes

A user with two operating systems on his computer often boots his computer and then completes another task. When he returns, his computer has booted the wrong operating system. You need to instruct the computer to wait longer so that the user can make a choice between operating systems.

1. Log on with your administrator account (the password is P@ssw0rd).

2. From the Start menu, right-click My Computer and select Properties.

3. In the System Properties dialog box, in the Advanced tab, in the Startup And Recovery section, click Settings.

4. In the Startup And Recovery dialog box, in the System Startup section, enter **99** in the Time To Display List Of Operating Systems text box, as shown below. Click OK.

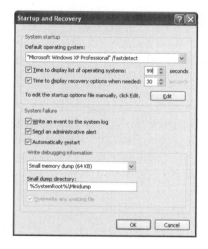

5. Close the System Properties dialog box.

EXERCISE 11.4: CONFIGURING PROGRAM COMPATIBILITY SETTINGS

Estimated completion time: 10 minutes

A user has recently upgraded from Microsoft Windows 95 to Windows XP, and one of her applications, a DOS program, is not working properly. You need to adjust the program compatibility settings to deal with the issue.

> **NOTE**   There would never be a circumstance using the Microsoft Office System under Windows XP in which you would need to alter the operating system compatibility settings. Most programs will not require configuring these settings. Exceptions will mostly be legacy programs designed for specific industries and older games.

1. Log on with your test account.

2. From the Start menu, select My Computer.

3. Browse to the folder C:\Program Files\Microsoft Office\Office11.

4. Locate and right-click the file EXCEL, and select Properties.

5. In the EXCEL Properties dialog box, in the Compatibility tab, in the Compatibility Mode section, select the Run This Program In Compatibility Mode For check box, and in the drop-down list, select Windows 95. Click OK.

6. Log off and log back on with your administrator account (the password is P@ssw0rd).

7. From the Start menu, select My Computer.

8. Browse to the folder C:\Program Files\Microsoft Office\Office11.

9. Locate and right-click the file EXCEL, and select Properties. Select the Compatibility tab.

QUESTION   Do compatibility settings extend beyond individual user accounts?

EXERCISE 11.5: USING REMOTE DESKTOP

Estimated completion time: 20 minutes

An executive is not too handy with computers, and he often requires your assistance. You have decided that it would be much easier if you could help him remotely, rather than having to sit at his computer each time he has a problem.

NOTE   The following exercise requires a partner. Steps 9 through 14 can be completed only by one partner at a time.

1. Log on with your administrator account (the password is P@ssw0rd).

2. From the Start menu, right-click My Computer and select Properties.

3. In the System Properties dialog box, in the Remote tab, in the Remote Desktop section, select the Allow Users To Connect Remotely To This Computer check box.

4. In the Remote Sessions message box, click OK. Click Select Remote Users.

5. In the Remote Desktop Users dialog box, click Add.

6. In the Select Users dialog box, in the Enter The Object Name To Select (Examples) text box, type **Administrator** and click Check Names. Click OK.

7. In the Remote Desktop Users dialog box, click OK.

8. In the System Properties dialog box, click OK.

NOTE   Steps 9 through 14 are to be completed by only one partner at this time.

9. From the Start menu, select All Programs, Accessories, Communications, and select Remote Desktop Connection.

10. In the Remote Desktop Connection dialog box, in the Computer text box, type **Computer*xx***, where **Computer*xx*** is the name of your partner's computer. Click Connect.

11. In the Log On To Windows dialog box, in the User Name text box, ensure that Administrator is entered. In the Password text box, type **P@ssw0rd**. Click OK.

12. Your partner's computer should lock, and you should see your partner's desktop.

13. On the Computer*xx* menu bar at the top of the screen, click the close button (it is an X).

14. In the Disconnect Windows Session message box, click OK.

15. Unlock your computer if it is locked.

> **NOTE** Steps 9 through 15 should now be performed again, with the roles of each partner reversed.

LAB REVIEW QUESTIONS

Estimated completion time: 15 minutes

1. What security attribute not configured for your student account is necessary to log on to a computer using Remote Desktop?

2. How can you configure Outlook to contain the same e-mail and other information across user accounts?

3. What file contains information telling the computer how to boot, which can be edited through the System Properties dialog box?

4. What happens to a computer concerning its availability locally when it is being used through Remote Desktop from another computer?

LAB CHALLENGE: RESOLVING FILE OWNERSHIP PROBLEMS AFTER AN UPGRADE TO WINDOWS XP

Estimated completion time: 25 minutes

A user complains that she cannot access files on a computer that was upgraded from Microsoft Windows NT 4 to Windows XP, both of which used the NTFS file system. She is using the correct user name and password.

All the data for the computer is stored on a separate partition from the operating system. When Windows XP was installed, the data partition was left alone. The user's access problems are occurring for a folder called Client Data located on the root of the data partition.

You need to research this problem in the Microsoft Knowledge base (hint: search for text strings such as "Windows XP", "Access is denied", "correct user name and password", and "NTFS File System", and look for "access is denied" in the article title. There is an article that describes the symptoms precisely. Find and read the article; it will explain how to fix the problem.

Before you attempt to fix the user's problem, you have decided to try to re-create the folder on your own system to see how you will solve it on the user's system.

Once you have your solution, take a screen shot of the dialog box and tab where the solution is implemented.

TROUBLESHOOTING LAB B
REVIEWING YOUR ENVIRONMENT

You are the primary technical support for a satellite office of Contoso Insurance. The branch has just increased its workforce by 50 percent, and you need to configure 5 new systems on the network.

Because the satellite operates independently from the rest of the company, and has only a small number of computers, the network is set up as a workgroup. The router used to connect the computers to the Internet runs Dynamic Host Configuration Protocol (DHCP). Domain Name System (DNS) requests are handled by a DNS server outside of the network, but internal to Contoso as a whole.

Although there are only 20 employees at the satellite office, you will be required to maintain a strict control over access to shared resources, since some groups need to be barred from certain shared resources.

Furthermore, each of the systems is configured with multiple user accounts, in part to improve security.

The environment suggests that you might have to deal with issues in the following areas:

- Network configuration and connectivity
- Access to shared resources
- Multiuser computers

Based on the information provided above and in Labs 8 through 11, answer the following questions:

1. How is security improved by implementing multiple accounts on each computer?

2. In what Microsoft Management Console (MMC) do you create user accounts?

3. What level of account is appropriate for ordinary users?

4. Given that there are 15 computers plus other nodes on the network, and the router offers DHCP, what makes sense as far as distributing Internet Protocol (IP) addresses to each of the systems?

5. What will happen if a computer is unable to obtain an IP address from DHCP?

6. What aspect of an APIPA IP address makes it obvious it was assigned using APIPA?

7. Should you configure the new systems to use simple file sharing?

8. What is the easiest way to ensure that a folder is private to a particular user?

9. When a computer is locked out because a user failed to use the correct password more times than policy allows, can you log on without a reboot with another user account?

10. When multiple users access Microsoft Office System products from different user accounts for the first time, is there any setup required?

LAB DEPENDENCIES

To complete this lab, you need to have completed the following:

- Lab 1, Exercises 1-1, 1-2, 1-5, and 1-6
- Lab 4, Exercises 4-1 and 4-2
- Lab 11, Exercise 11-1
- If you completed Lab 8, then you need to complete the Before you Begin section of Lab 9, 10, or 11.

CHANGING THE COMPUTER CONFIGURATION

In this portion of the lab, your classmates or your instructor will change the computer configuration to create problems to troubleshoot in the next section. Two break scenarios are presented. Your instructor will decide which computers will be subject to which break scenarios.

TROUBLESHOOTING

In this portion of the lab, you must resolve problems created in the "Changing the Computer Configuration" section.

Break Scenario 1

You are the primary technical support for all users at a satellite office of Contoso Insurance. Maria Hammond, a graphic designer, reports several problems with her computer. For convenience, pretend that your student account is Maria Hammond's user account. John Doe's account will be used as an example of a Power User account.

1. Her first problem is that since the network was renovated, she has lost her Internet connection.

2. Her second problem is that once the first problem is solved, the other office computers do not appear when she clicks View Workgroup Computers in My Network Places.

3. Third, a folder called Financials on your partner's computer that is supposed to be shared locally and on the network is not available to all network users.

4. Fourth, although all users are able to access files on a shared network resource called Scheduling, some are unable to create folders in it.

Steps for Diagnosing the Problems

1. See if you can access *http://www.microsoft.com* over the Internet. Run Network Diagnostics from the Help and Support Center. Read the report and pinpoint the problems.

2. Check for connectivity to other computers by using ping. If connectivity exists, run **net config workstation** at the command line.

3. Determine what network users are able and unable to access the Scheduling folder. This involves accessing the folder from another computer. On the computer containing the folder, check the sharing settings assigned to the folder while logged on with an administrator account.

4. By logging on with accounts with different security privileges (User, Power User, and so on), see which groups are unable to create new folders in the Scheduling folder. Check the NTFS Permissions to see what privileges are given to what groups.

Problem Diagnosis

1. DHCP is not enabled, and an incorrect IP address and default gateway are configured.

2. The workgroup name has been misspelled.

3. The Power Users group has explicitly been denied access to the network share. Local power users are able to access the folder because sharing settings do not affect local users.

4. The Power Users group has been denied the NTFS Permission to create new folders in the Scheduling folder.

Steps to Repair the Problems

1. In the Internet Protocol (TCP/IP) Properties dialog box, select Obtain An IP Address Automatically. Also select Obtain DNS Server Address Automatically. At a command prompt, run ipconfig /release and ipconfig / renew.

2. In the Computer Name tab of the System Properties dialog box, click Change. In the Computer Name Changes dialog box, in the Member Of section, in the Workgroup text box, type **WORKGROUP**.

3. In the Shared Documents folder, in the Properties dialog box for the Financials folder, in the Sharing tab, click Permissions. Remove the Power Users group from the Group Or User Names list.

4. In the Properties dialog box for the Scheduling folder, in the Security tab, click Advanced. In the Permissions Entries list, select Power Users in the Name column, and click Edit. Clear the Deny check box for the Create Folders/Append Data permission.

Break Scenario 2

You are the primary technical support for all users at a satellite office of Contoso Insurance. Maria Hammond, a graphic designer, reports several problems with her computer. For convenience, pretend that your student account is Maria Hammond's user account. John Doe's account will be used as an example of a Power User account.

1. Her first problem is that if she accidentally types in the wrong password, she is locked out of her computer for a full day (24 hours).

2. Her second problem is that she doesn't have connectivity to the Internet.

3. Third, although she is able to see others' computers in My Network Places, they cannot see her computer.

4. She recently had technical support transfer her old e-mail messages from her old computer to her current computer. Because the network was not yet functional, they transferred her e-mails on a CD. When she starts Outlook, there is an error message and the program closes when she clicks OK to dismiss it.

Steps for Diagnosing the Problems

1. Try entering an incorrect password for a user account twice and see what happens. Use the test account. Check the account lockout settings in the Local Security Settings console.

2. Try accessing *http://www.microsoft.com*. Check connectivity to other computers on the network using ping. Run Network Diagnosis from the Help And Support Center.

3. Check connectivity going out and coming in by pinging another computer on the network from her computer. Given that her computer can access the network, but the network cannot access her computer, consider what feature of Windows would restrict incoming IP traffic.

4. Run Outlook logged on with her account and read the error message.

Problem Diagnosis

1. The lockout policy is set to lock out users for a day after one bad logon attempt.

2. The DNS server is set to the wrong IP address.

3. Her computer is running Internet Connection Firewall (ICF).

4. When a file is copied to a CD, the read-only attribute is set. When her PST file was copied from the CD to her computer, the read-only attribute was not removed.

Steps to Repair the Configuration

1. In the Internet Protocol (TCP/IP) Properties dialog box, either set the Preferred DNS Server to 10.1.1.200 or select Obtain DNS Server Address Automatically.

2. With your administrator account, in the Local Security Settings console, in the Account Lockout policy node, change the Account Lockout Threshold to 5 and the Account Lockout Duration to 30 minutes.

3. In the Advanced tab of the Local Area Connection Properties dialog box, clear the Protect My Computer And Network By Limiting Or Preventing Access To This Computer From The Internet check box.

4. Clear the Read-Only check box in the Properties dialog box of her PST file in the General tab. The path for the file will appear in the error message.